CU00696001

A present from the CCF committee
Thanks to a generous donation, we are
able to send each of our members this
free gift.
www.carerschristianfellowship.org.uk

ARE YOU LISTENING?

Carole Crossley

Jesus Joy Publishing

First Published and printed in Great Britain in 2019 by
Jesus Joy Publishing, a division of Eklegein Ltd.

ISBN 978-1-90797-155-6

Jesus Joy Publishing
A division of Eklegein Ltd
www.jesusjoypublishing.co.uk
260319

Acknowledgements

I would like to thank my dear friends - Alison, Mary and Wesley who kindly allowed me to send them the readings on a daily basis and have been a great encouragement to me. Also my son, Steve, who is a never-ending source of love and support.

About the Author

I had a Christian upbringing, but like many teenagers, I left God behind when I thought that I didn't need Him. After a failed first marriage, I reached rock bottom and began to search for God. That was over thirty years ago and although my life hasn't been a smooth passage, God has been my constant Rock. God doesn't promise to prevent problems in His children's lives, but He does promise to help us with them.

After thirty-three years of marriage to my second husband, his health has deteriorated and that means that he needs full time care. We have one wonderful son and it is very difficult for Steve and I to watch this gentle man, who is disappearing before our eyes, day by day. It feels worse than a bereavement.

It is during the difficult times that I have realised how much I need God. I know that he is always there with me, waiting for me to invite him to get involved. I often wonder why it sometimes takes me so long to remember that.

This devotional was born out of my great sadness, after I reached out to God in my anguish. I began to write it during the night just before Christmas 2017. I believe it is inspired by God and It is written as if He is speaking directly to the reader, in the same way that God spoke to me.

It became all-consuming and has helped me to grow in my faith as I searched God's word, trying to find passages of scripture to complement the messages that He had given to me. I needed three attempts to pass English language so writing this devotional was an endorsement to me that I was really hearing from God and that He can use anyone. I would just pick up a pen and write, I had little recollection of what I had written and the whole task, excluding editing, took three months. Indeed, God uses the most unlikely people.

I am grateful to 'Jesus Joy Publishing' for being prepared to take a chance on this devotional.

Foreword

When I went to Bible College in the mid-60s, I was a very young Christian. We were taught personal discipline in our daily walk with Christ. One of these was what was known as 'The Quiet Time.' I hadn't a clue what it meant. At that time it meant an hour in your own room with God before breakfast. You had to learn daily reading of the Bible assisted by Daily Readings/helps mainly through Scripture Union Publications. I must confess I sometimes found myself asleep on my knees when the breakfast bell rang!

How times have changed! Quiet Time is now 'snatching time' as you people go to work and CDs, mp3s and iPads /phones spill spew out verses of scripture to read and meditate upon throughout the day. A whole generation is caught up in instant communication and it leaves little time for digestion. It creates a generation that lives on 'sound bites'. That's the emerging Christian world we are living in and it's such a challenge.

These daily, brief notes are sound bites for those in a hurry. However, the reflections and thoughts were not quarried out in a hurry. They were 'dug out' in the rough of life where Christ is and where His promises are chiselled into the present day Christian's life. The writer of these notes knows the struggles of failure, the sadness of loss, the frustration of unanswered prayer and the daily battle with self. She has known God opening up new channels of communication through poetry and personal discoveries of her Lord's lovely ways.

I am delighted to add this word of encouragement to her and all those who will read these daily notes of love. May you take time, listen and maybe write your own thoughts as these become triggers in your mind to lead you into a deeper walk of faith.

In it all 'to God be the glory!'

Rev Wesley Loane,

Part time Chaplain and weekly Preacher (anywhere!)

Contents

January

✝ *1st January*

You have no need to concern yourself about tomorrow. The urgency in your life can hold you back from My blessings. Leave even the smallest event with Me, I will plan the fine details. Just show up as expected and all will be well.

The strife you feel by over-planning causes us both heartache. My control is rejected and disaster occurs only when you go it alone. If you ask for My help, I will guide you, even amidst those mishaps.

Proverbs 3:6

> *"Seek His will in all you do and He will direct your path."*

✝ 2nd January

Always I am waiting for you. I wish to be involved in your life, wake up and think of Me. I do not present you with a smooth passage, but My presence will always ensure the best outcome.

Never take umbrage when your plans go awry; it could be that your intentions were flawed. I see that to which you are blind. Trust that I always know best. Place your hand in Mine and allow My will to unfold.

Psalm 55:22

"Give your burdens to the Lord and He will take care of you. He will not permit the Godly to slip and fall."

✝ 3rd January

Don't wrestle any more with things you can't change. Rise above the now and keep coming into My presence. It is when we commune together that my work can be done. I constantly lead you in little, unknown ways.

My hands are wide open with gifts, things not appreciated by man, but valuable gifts from Me to you. Take all that I offer and share it. The hurt and lonely souls come from Me, look after them. Look for the treasures I give you and respond with love, My love.

Prayer

> *Father, forgive me for taking so much in my life for granted. Help me to care for Your people, with a glad and humble heart. Whatever you have given me, make me willing to share it. Thank you that in You, I might be able to help change the circumstances of someone in need. Change my heart to be ready to move when You ask it. In Jesus name, Amen.*

✝ 4th January

I enfold you in My arms where you are safe. Don't let fear spoil your future. I will never allow misfortune to take you under. Each precious day that I am with you, is a good day. Rise above these earthly events, nothing you do can change them; but keep trying to see the light beyond the darkness and follow Me with trust.

One day heaven and earth will be one and the hurts of this world will be no more. It is then your actions in the world will be counted and the good you have done will be proclaimed.

Isaiah 41:10

"Don't be afraid for I am with you. Do not be dismayed for I am your God. I will strengthen you. I will help you. I will uphold you with my victorious right hand."

✝ 5th January

In the darkness of this time, I am the only brightness. Focus your sights on Me. Never waver from My track, place your feet assuredly upon My path until the goal can be reached. The time is urgent and I don't want you to deviate.

Search, search and search again, until you find Me. Take nothing in this world for granted, My power will draw you into an intimate understanding of My ways. Gradually the light will become so bright that you will wonder how you missed it.

John 8:12

"Jesus said to the people, 'I am the light of the world.
If you follow me, you won't be stumbling through the
darkness, because you will have the light that leads to
life.'"

✝ 6th January

Oh My child, now is the time to begin to leave the things of this world behind you. Move swiftly into My design, don't look to the side, but focus ahead. Each step you take will be a desirable move with Me. The dusty corners will be cleaned out. It takes time, but be expectant, be vigilant, be ready.

My methods are the one thing that eventually your heart will desire. I am able to change everything in the blink of My eye. The dark pastures you have been travelling are going to change. The unguided route will be no more. Steadfastly and constantly, together we will move forward.

Luke 9:57-58

> *"As they were walking along someone said to Jesus, 'I will follow you wherever you go.' But Jesus replied, 'Foxes have dens to live in and birds have nests, but I the son of man have no home of my own, not even a place to lay my head.'"*

Jesus wants to make his home in you.

✝ 7th January

Make haste to transform your lives, leave nothing to chance. Study My Word with a pure heart and I will give you clear understanding. During different seasons of your lives, I will open and reveal the scriptures. Reaffirm your love for Me and commit regular time for us to grow closer.

Do not feel anguish when I am silent, give with obedient faith, all your worries and concerns. The prayers of a righteous soul cause heaven to spring into action. My timing is not as you desire. Learn patience and always be expectant. Today I will do a good thing in you.

Habakkuk 2:3

> *"But these things I plan won't happen right away.*
> *Slowly, steadily, surely, the time approaches when the*
> *vision will be fulfilled. If it seems slow wait patiently, for*
> *it will surely take place. It will not be delayed."*

✝ 8th January

Each member of My body is an asset. You complement each other as you work like the mechanism of a finely tuned machine. Your gifts are many and given as needed within My Kingdom. Develop those skills which are a blessing from Me. Use them regularly.

If each part were to operate as one, the complexity of working together would be made simple. These acts of trust would bring a unity of love, which would spread around each nation. The result would be everlasting harmony.

Ephesians 4:16

> *"Under his direction the whole body is fitted together perfectly. As each part does its own special work, it helps the other parts grow, so that the whole body is healthy and growing and full of love."*

✝ 9th January

Prepare, plan, read, study. I have given you the tools and the necessary elements to glean more from My Word. The next step must come from you. Open your minds to let Me teach you. Each one of My children is unique and special to Me, and each one of you will have a personal, intimate relationship with Me. It will be like no other. It will grow to be compulsive, it will outshine all human communications.

But action on your part is needed, so pray, ask and again expect. Look out for My messages which will come in a variety of ways. Be receptive, I will enable you to understand when I speak. We will grow closer together until we are one.

Prayer

Lord help me to truly recognise the variety of ways in which you speak. Increase my awareness and confidence to know when I'm hearing from you. Protect me from myself and the destruction of wrong paths. I want to be open to your Spirit changing me. Use me Lord - I am the clay.

Amen.

✝ *10th January*

The things of society can begin to cloud your judgement. Go back time and again to My Word. I will open the truth to reveal the things of heaven. Always confer with Me about minor, as well as major issues, not only in your own private world, but also in the wider view of nations.

I am being increasingly removed from every conceivable area of daily life. I am being put into compartments and used only for show. My back seat is a lonely place and I long for My people. Continue to include Me. A time is coming when I need you to stand up and be counted. Be on your guard, the days are shortening.

Thought

> *We are allowing political correctness to gain the upper hand and it has resulted in God being taken out of so many areas in our society. As Christians we need to make our voices heard. The headlines are proof that by allowing Christianity to be watered down, there is an increase in the powers of darkness. Satan creeps stealthily into our schools, in our relationships and he even tries to get into our churches. Are we going to let him?*

✝ 11th January

My love will be powerless in your life without your co-operation. Allow your senses to be in line with My thoughts. This will only happen if you spend quality time with Me. I will put a longing into your heart for this, so heed it.

As each precious minute with Me passes, I will amplify these moments to mean much more than mere time. Jealously guard this time with Me! I will reward your commitment by opening up, to show you, not only your life's purpose, but how I will help you to achieve it.

Psalm 37:4-7

> *"Take delight in the Lord, and he will give you your hearts desires. Commit everything you do to the Lord. Trust him, and he will help you. He will make your innocence as clear as the dawn, and the justice of your cause will shine like the noonday sun. Be still in the presence of the Lord and wait for him to act."*

✝ *12th January*

When darkness falls in your life, do not allow it to cloud your judgement. Allow Me to be all things to you. Firmly decide to grant Me control. I take time to amend the little things that in due course would counteract so much to come against you.

But remember, you are an individual and I have given you free will. I am always aware when you go down the wrong track, but it is YOU who must make the decision to turn around. My grace is always sufficient to protect you.

Romans 3:24-25

"Yet not God in his gracious kindness, declares us not guilty. We are made right with God when we believe that Jesus shed his blood, sacrificing his life for us."

✝ *13th January*

Come back to Me, My child, especially when your heart is full and you think you are sinking. I will never turn you away. No matter how much sin you have allowed into your life, your iniquities are never more than I will forgive.

I understand your human frailties, I know how your mind works and yet I love you. I yearn for each of My children to stay close to Me. It is then that I can cleanse and heal their hurts. Do not condemn yourselves or each other. My deep desire is for My love to stabilise the world.

Thessalonians 3:3

> *"But the Lord is faithful, he will make you strong and guard you from the evil one."*

✝ *14th January*

You and I will have an eternal relationship. What happens in this life is a mere speck in a vast universe. Never forget that I see the longings of your secret heart. My wish is to give to you and give again; but when I note the error in your thinking, I will intervene via your conscience.

My children have the available counsel of My Word. Read it often with a prayerful heart and be ready to receive a new understanding. The scriptures are steadfast with a clear, enlightening guidance, to assist you in every direction. Allow the gentle nudge from My Spirit to ensure your feet are on firm ground.

2 Timothy 3:16

> *"All scripture is inspired by God and is useful to teach us what is true and make us realise what is wrong in our lives. It straightens us out and teaches us to do what is right."*

✝ *15th January*

Come before Me and listen; so often My children come out of obligation. Yes, you may be committed to Me, but we still need quality time together. Sometimes I just want you to sit and wait; plunge into My Spirit during these times. Let Me penetrate your heart and soul.

Give Me all of your attention. Capture those thoughts that cause you to stray away from My presence. It will take practice but I will help you. Enjoy learning from Me, come without preconceived ideas. All My children are different and special and I will reach each of you in a unique way.

Prayer

Lord, by the power of Your Spirit, I rebuke all my rogue thoughts and I bow my head in reverence before You.
Make me open to Your leading, aware of Your voice and ready to enjoy being still in Your presence. Amen.

✝ *16th January*

Come and confess that which is bitter and resentful in your life. Relationships will often fail, especially when 'self' becomes too important. I know your human nature is selfish, but I have given you the resources to overcome.

My Son took all of your sin upon Himself, but without My conviction, you would be unaware. It will be an ongoing battle, but My Spirit is changing you. I empower you to recognise quickly that which is wrong. Your speed to confess will save you.

1 John: 1:8-9

"If we say we have no sin, we are only fooling ourselves and refusing to accept the truth. But if we confess our sins to him, he is faithful and just to forgive us and to cleanse us from every wrong."

✝ 17th January

Never will I ask you to do something which is too much for you. It is always My power that enables you. I want you to recognise this; it will give you confidence to comply with My wishes. Trust that I know your heart and you and I will move mountains together in My Kingdom.

I will build you up in your dreams - they are based on My firm foundation and structure for your life. Do not doubt that which is achievable with Me.

Isaiah 25:1

> *"O Lord I will honour and praise your name, for you are my God. You do such wonderful things! You planned them long ago and now you have accomplished them."*

✝ 18th January

You accomplish many things each day; by completing a task, you 'have' achieved. What seems mundane to the world is important to Me. I build your character on such things. Discipline is important in the little, seemingly insignificant things in order for the construction of My Kingdom.

All My children are key players. I want you to work each day in obedience to Me. Do not think that what you do is unimportant; many inconsequential events are the building blocks that I use for greater things. Be in awe of My design and yield to your part; be ever-ready when I call and commission you.

Acts 20:22

"And now I am going to Jerusalem, drawn there irresistibly by the Holy Spirit, not knowing what awaits me."

✝ 19th January

Let Me encourage you, My child, so that you won't be tempted to quit. Sometimes when you meet opposition, you wonder if you have got it wrong and you have misheard Me. Trust your instinct (which comes from Me), that you are being led by My voice.

Again, don't despair; if I appear to be silent, your free will keeps Me from any interference. I will only speak into your situation when the danger would be too much for you. Draw again on My promise that I will never leave you. Keep track of life's happenings - they will confirm that I am with you and you are never alone. I love you, My child.

Romans 8:28

"And we know that God causes everything to work together for the good of those who love God and are called according to his purpose for them."

✝ *20th January*

Fear is a stronghold and its grip is the devil's greatest success. My Word continually emphasises 'do not fear'. I don't expect you to never feel fear, but I don't want you to give in to it! Together we can work through your fear. Trust in Me is paramount. I am always pleased by your trust because I realise your circumstances colour your mind towards the future.

The unknown and its eventualities are beyond anyone's control but Mine. Step out in faith! If you have invited My authority into your life, then trust My sovereignty to guide you, overseeing all you do. I can and do influence your situation so that My purpose can take effect.

Deuteronomy 31:8

> *"Do not be afraid or discouraged, for the Lord is the one who goes before you. He will be with you, he will neither fail you nor forsake you."*

✝ *21st January*

Let Me fine-tune you to manage your time better. You can clean up many areas of your life, and dispose of some completely. I yearn for you to spend time with Me as a committed child of God. I wait for you to wait on Me as I am preparing you for greater things. Time managed is a blessing from Me and will always benefit you.

Your lives have become cluttered and I want you to learn to say No! Some of your tasks are done with an element of resentment; that is because it takes up time which I would prefer you to spend with Me. If each of My children would start each day by asking for My guidance, together we would accomplish much more. I will not dominate, but I want you to enjoy our communion together.

Jeremiah 29:11-14

"For I know the plans I have for you says the Lord. They are plans for good and not disaster, to give you a future and a hope. In those days when you pray I will listen. If you look for me in earnest, you will find me, when you seek me I will be found by you."

✝ *22nd January*

I will make our time together productive. If you come with a pure heart, My plans for you will unfold. If you come with a battered heart, I will gently repair the damage. Speak truth to Me, tell Me what you would tell no other. My lips are forever sealed with your secrets; I already know them but I want you to open up to Me, My child, and leave nothing out.

It is only when you are completely honest that I can begin to work. I will show you the road ahead and give you the ability to combat all that grieves you. Sometimes you have made wrong choices - choices that have hurt you and others; that is what free will has done. When you turn to Me in your despair, you release My power and I have the freedom to help you.

Matthew 11:27-28

> *"My father has given me authority over everything, no one really knows the son except the father and no one really knows the father except the son and those to who the son chooses to reveal him. Come to me, all you who are weary and carry heavy burdens and I will give you rest."*

✝ 23rd January

Imagine your life is like a lake; if someone throws in a pebble, the ripple spreads out to the edge. When I am at the centre of your life, the tremors of My love will flow outwardly, causing new ripples to begin, as they touch others.

My love will spread from you. As an example, the shock waves will be caught up and the blessing which I first began in you, My child, will touch and spread to others. Their lives in turn will be transformed as they too are soaked in My love. A harvest will be gathered by your actions.

Mark 12:30-31

> *"And you shall love the Lord your God with all your heart and with all your soul and with all your mind and with all your strength. The second is this, you shall love your neighbour as yourself. There is no other commandment greater than these."*

✝ 24th January

As you learn from Me, your heart will align with Mine. We are on an adventure together, you as you change and grow in My likeness, and Me as I watch you complete the new tasks that I set for you. When they feel daunting, remember, I am only a prayer away. Never will I expect you to accomplish anything without My input. It is up to you how often you invite Me to be a part of that.

I am always ready and eager to assist My children, but in order to grow, you must bring your free will into line with My will. I never teach by punishment but rather I chasten you out of love. Whatever you do without, will be for your ultimate benefit. It is during your trials that I am able to teach you effectively, because you are vulnerable and more available to Me. The trials that happen are never sent from Me, but I do use them for good.

Psalm 30:2-3

"O Lord my God I cried out to you for help and you restored my health. You brought me up from the grave. O Lord you kept me falling into the pit of death."

✝ *25th January*

I am always aware when you need Me, and it pleases Me when you call on My name. I want you to grow in stature, to always have confidence in Me. Be bold - I have given you the gifts and necessary tools to handle things. Go in My strength, with the certain knowledge that I am with you. Your actions during some dire circumstances, will endorse My presence in your life to others - those who don't yet know Me.

Always be aware of your behaviour, you are My representative and they will judge Me by your actions. I have blessed you with great responsibility in My Kingdom. Include Me, and I will be effective in your weakness. Increase the trust you have in Me, even when I am silent.

Jeremiah 17:7-8

"But blessed is the one who trusts in the Lord, whose confidence is in him. They will be like a tree planted by the water that sends its roots out by a stream. It does not fear when heat comes; it is always green. It has no worries in a year of draught and never fails to bear fruit."

✝ *26th January*

Be in no doubt that I chose you, just as I chose Jacob over Esau. I have made My home in you; your body is a temple and you are obligated to take care of it. You are afforded a privilege by My presence; take every opportunity to honour Me. Now that My Spirit lives in you, your values will be different. Each of My children are equally special to Me, and I do not have favourites amongst you.

Each of you meets Me on a different level which is dependant on your journey and the frequency of your stops. Let us enjoy our time together. In your desire to know Me better, I will reveal different aspects of My character. The one I want you to be most familiar with is My love for you and for all living creatures. Take care of My world - it is very precious to Me.

Ephesians 2:4-5

"But God being rich in mercy, because of the great love with which he loved us, even when we were dead in our trespasses, made us alive together with Christ - by grace you have been saved."

✝ 27th January

I love to laugh - did you know that about Me? My Son received His love of celebrations from Me. This world has so much misery which increases continually. I don't want My children to be downhearted about the things they are unable to change. Let Me remind you of joy and how to leave those desperate situations with Me. I motivate My people to respond, but when individually, you have attempted all you are able to, you must trust that I am acting.

Your righteous indignation is good, but don't let events drag you down; sorrow will deplete your effectiveness for Me and joy is one of My blessings. Look for the fun side of every situation and I will give you a buoyant mood.

Prayer

When I have done all I can to ease the distress of others, protect me from being sucked down into their pain. Show me how to maintain a joyful heart, that comes from within, and bless me with your peace that surpasses all understanding. Amen.

✝ *28th January*

You will have many new beginnings during this year, so be thankful for My forgiveness. There is no condemnation for your mistakes, just come to Me quickly when you have made one. I know that this destructive world gives you a constant battle; but as you allow Me to change you and give you My strength, then each step you take with Me will be a victory. Do not pass judgement on others - that must always be left to Me. Never look beyond your life into the life of another, unless I am looking with you.

Accept that each one of you is different and I have made many patterns. Don't look down on each other, not because of appearance, moral conduct or any actions which are unlike your own. My will is that you live in peaceful harmony with all men and all nations. Accept authority without petty grumbles, but with gladness of heart, you can do that which My Word permits. Listen to My Spirit, open My Word and be ready to act on My leadership.

Philippians 4:13

"*For I can do everything with the help of Christ who gives me the strength I need.*"

✝ *29th January*

I value your time more than your works. My Kingdom needs both, in order for success. Heed that nudge I often give you to visit the sick and lonely. My love will grow wherever you touch others. You must come into My presence often, not just on Sundays. I patiently wait for you to remember Me - I should be your first port of call. I want to enter all areas of your life, nothing is too insignificant for My attention - nothing!

There is a thread that connects you to Me. That thread is unbreakable, but do not stretch it too far. I want you to truly believe that I love you, and you are made righteous by the blood of My Son. When you invited Me into your life, His sacrifice was made perfect and the Angels' voices resounded in heaven. Many of My children fail to understand and feel His sacrifice deeply; it is the first step to a real relationship with Me.

Prayer

> *Father thank you for revealing, in Jesus, your great love for Me. Help me in the enemy's constant battle for my soul. Help me to always listen and be aware when you speak to my innermost being. Protect me from all outside influences that would damage that which you are building up. Put a ready forgiveness in my heart as with my willing consent you are changing me to be more like Jesus. Amen.*

✝ 30th January

My arms are always here to cushion you in life's storms. Just because you are My loving child doesn't mean you will never face adversity, but it does mean that you will never face it alone. During times of strife and stress, I want to carry you - please let Me. I want you to totally rely on Me. Many will say that you have blind faith - but that would be faith without evidence. You have the evidence of the resurrection.

Your prayers release My power into the 'eye of the storm'; be patient in waiting for Me to act. My timing is perfect and I will move mountains for you. Look back often, and note the times you can see My hand at work. If I say No, it is because I have something better for you. Trust Me as we become closer. Sometimes you must act when I call, so search for My will. I have many blessings waiting for you!

Ephesians 2:8-9

"God saved you by his special favour when you believed. And you can't take credit for this; it is a gift from God. Salvation is not a reward for the good things we have done, so none of us can boast about it, for we are God's masterpiece. He has created us anew in Christ Jesus, so that we can do the good things he planned for us long ago."

✝ *31st January*

Don't run away from My voice. I do not want you to have to spend time inside the whale as Jonah did; that would grieve My Spirit and also, ultimately, you. So much time is wasted by My children being disobedient. I will not punish you! That is never My method. I will teach you, but only in a manner that will help you. You are at a crossroads and the signs point in different directions. Some say 'sorrow', some say 'stress', but you must follow the ones that say 'Jesus', for those will bring you to Me.

You will find those signs between the pages of My Word, and then we will be on the route together. If, My child, you are a new Christian, I will gently nurture you. If you are already on the road, I will encourage you. If you are lost on your journey, I will bring you back. I see all that is shut away from the rest of the world. My Son intercedes on your behalf, and He is the connection that you will need.

John 14:6-7

"I am the way, the truth and the life. No one can come to the father except through me. If you had known who I am, then you would have known who my father is. From now on you know him and have seen him!"

February

✝ 1st February

Come, I will teach you self-control. You do not need to be a slave to that chocolate bar or that extra glass of addictive beverage. I will be your comfort. Those of My children who have emotional pain should use Me as a prop. I can take you places where your mind will be so strengthened against worldly desires that they will fade into insignificance.

Learn to divert your thoughts away from self-gratification which is only momentary. Call on My name so I can come to strengthen you in your weaknesses. You are rich in My gifts but I don't like over indulgence. In Me you have all you need. A clean and healthy mind will lead to a clean and healthy body. The irritants in your body come from an imbalance. Focus on Me, making your thoughts at one with higher things and your body will automatically fall into line.

Proverbs 25:28

"A person without self-control is as defenceless as a city with broken down walls."

✝ 2nd February

Draw consistently from My provision. Don't you know how I long to give to you? Each tiny thing is a spiritual or material gift from Me. Relax into the knowledge that I will take care of you. Come to Me often with a thankful heart and I will cause the joy of giving to grow within you. Look all around you for signs of need and respond with quick delight as you share all I have given.

Your spiritual gifts will bless those around you. Ask Me for guidance and wisdom as you use them. Understand the importance of gentleness. It is a harsh reality that My children are needy; I made you this way and I long to fill the gap in your lives. Yes, I like an independent spirit as long as that spirit has its foundation in Me and a reliance on Me, to constantly return for My leadership.

2 Corinthians 8:12

> *"If you are really eager to give, it isn't important how much you are able to give. God wants you to give what you have, not what you don't have?"*

✝ 3rd February

Give and give again, the amount is unimportant - the desire is what I look for. Gather around and learn from the Master who has given everything. I never tire of providing for you but I want you to behave responsibly. You, My child, have a moral obligation to save and protect for the future - but this must not be done at the expense of someone in need. Whatever you share with others, I will replenish your measure.

Never be concerned that your own supply will run out. Always imagine yourself in their situation and however you would like them to treat you, do likewise. I will reward each kindness. Do your giving quietly, without fuss, retreating from attention. Remember, My dear child, I will see all you do!

2 Corinthians 9:8

"And God will generously provide all you need. Then you will always have everything you need and plenty left over to share with others."

✝ *4th February*

I want you to share not only your monetary wealth but also your time and other gifts. The character I am nurturing in you is for you to be like My Son. Do not look for your kindness to be reciprocated. Even the tiniest act of goodness from you will never go unnoticed in heaven. I keep a record of these deeds and it will cause others to be drawn to Me when they look at you. The joy experienced in heaven by these acts would amaze you.

When that 'still small voice' speaks into your heart, I want you to acknowledge that it is Me you are hearing. Hurry and spontaneously gear up for action. When you feel low and despondent, the best medicine is to help someone else. I will uplift your heart as you in turn uplift others. The kindness you administer reveals My love. Thank you.

Luke 6:38

> *"If you give you will receive. Your gift will return to you in full measure, pressed down, shaken together to make room for more and running over. Whatever you use in giving - large or small - it will be used to measure what is given back to you."*

✝ *5th February*

Do you understand what I mean when I say you are made in My own image? I do not concern myself with outward, physical appearances. I can see under the surface deep into your soul. All My children are lovely to Me. The world judges by youthful beauty, but I can see beyond and it takes a lifetime for Me to change you on the inside. The more time you spend with a willingness to learn from Me, the quicker the process will become. You are righteous in Christ.

The youth cannot contemplate that the years will age their bodies. In My Son, your innermost being will be as one who is young. Just as a child is trusting and accepting, soaking up new things like a sponge, you - who have loved Me back - will soak up My love and become a new person.

2 Corinthians 5:17

"What this means is that those who become Christians, become new persons. They are not the same any more, for the old is gone. A new life has begun."

✝ 6th February

Beware that whatever you offer to Me, to bring change in you or your circumstances, may have been a nudge from My Spirit. I do not go back on My promises, so if you invite My input, expect it. Because I have given you free will, I often need a contingency plan. These plans only come into operation when you have strayed from the original path. I will work out an event to change your course.

My timing isn't the same as yours, I am never in a rush. Sometimes My children need to experience their own way, before coming around to Mine. I allow these learning curves in order to build up your experience and character. You will eventually realise the error of your ways and we will begin again. Come quickly with your mistakes and ask My forgiveness. As a parent easily forgives a child, so it will be with us.

Psalm 139:24

"Search me O God and know my heart; test me and know my anxious thoughts. Point out anything in me which offends you and lead me along the path of life everlasting."

✝ *7th February*

Can you see the pain caused to Me when you have doubts about My existence? Once I'm invited to come into your life, I live in you! What can cause these doubts, My child? I have granted each one of you an inquiring mind, and if you truly search for Me, you will find Me! You question why I allow such terrible world and social events. Believe this, My angels and My Son are in a constant battle to combat these horrors and safeguard people's souls.

I need more steadfast Christian soldiers to help in the fight. I do not want to spend time with questions that are not for this life. Your faith is all I ask. I do not want you to go off at a tangent. Good debate on spiritual issues has its place, but it is more valuable to believe that I work diligently in this world against the powers of darkness.

Prayer

Father forgive me for doubting You. I believe in Your goodness. The situations in the world cause me to question why You permit these things. Help me when I waver and lose sight of Your hand at work. I believe that You teach and strengthen me as I witness the dire circumstances of others. Help me to hold onto my trust in You. Amen.

✝ *8th February*

Don't use your secret mistakes to gain sympathy from others by twisting the true details. I do not condemn My children having forgiven their sins, but you must not use them to justify your actions. Some of you have done dreadful things; some may have been done before you came to life in me. Remember that I cannot live in an unclean vessel and when I forgave you, My Son's sacrifice saved you and I forgot your sins.

Turn away now and accept My forgiveness! Let Me comfort you, accept My salvation and remember it no more. If society makes judgements on some issue that you have been guilty of, remember My words. There is nothing that My children can't bring to Me with. It is an act of trust when you confide your darkest secrets to Me. Let Me comfort and heal. You are a child of God.

Acts 13:38-39

"In this man Jesus there is forgiveness for your sins.
Everyone who believes in him is freed from all guilt and
declared right with God."

✝ *9th February*

Don't you know that I yearn to be in your life, but when you worry you are excluding Me? Come, with even the smallest of your concerns, but please, when you ask for My help, trust that I will give it. Many of you come in fervent prayer, inviting Me to get involved, then you take it back; so what should relieve your tension doesn't, just as if you hadn't asked Me.

It is during these trials that My power is made perfect. Your part is to give it to Me, do whatever I ask of you, and trust Me to do the rest. I will be at the centre with you, I know what you are feeling. You will grow in Me when you watch My hand at work. I care about you!

Exodus 14:13

"But Moses told the people, 'Don't be afraid, just stand where you are and watch the Lord rescue you. The Egyptians that you see today will never be seen again. The Lord himself will fight for you. You won't have to lift a finger in your defence.'"

✝ *10th February*

I want to protect your health from the stresses in your life and this world. It is a fact that they exist. You and I can work on them together but this will require you to make some changes. First of all, I want you to look at your daily routine and I will help you to prioritise. I know that this won't be simple. Write down the things that you have got to accomplish each week, then narrow down the necessities for each day. Come to Me in prayer with your list and I will help you to manage your time.

Sometimes you are stressed by events that you have no control over. Each one of you will react and be affected to different degrees by worry. Let Me help to smooth your path. Speak My name often into situations you are concerned about and watch and be encouraged by My involvement. Draw continually on My peace which is readily available to all My children.

John 16:33

> *"I have told you all this so that you may have peace in Me. Here on earth you will have many trials and sorrows. But take heart because I have overcome the world."*

✝ *11th February:*

Do not be complicit in each other's sins. When a trust that concerns you is shared, bring it straight to Me. Do not judge but love them through the heartache. My children often go astray; the temptations of this world are numerous and I understand all of your weaknesses - but I do not condone them.

I will act in each situation at the appropriate time. I am concerned with damage limitation but I am unable to turn a blind eye. The corruption of a soul grows ever more when things are hidden. Help Me to bring all things into the light by asking Me to intervene.

Proverbs 3:5-6

"Trust in the Lord with all your heart; do not not depend on your own understanding. Seek his will in all you do, and he will direct your paths."

✝ *12th February*

No matter what road you are on, don't ever feel that you are alone. My attention is always on you, even when you are withdrawn from Me. I want our fellowship together to be smooth, but there will always be bumps on the way. Sometimes the bumps are problems you are unable to get around; sometimes the problems are so large you can't even see over them. I don't want you to hold these things inside, they will expand beyond what is reasonable.

I can disperse them but only if you want to include Me. There is always going to be some kind of hump to slow your progress. The secret is to go over them with Me, as alone you will keep sliding down the steep sides. My Word will give you guidance when you are troubled. Open the pages often and My wisdom will be revealed.

Psalm 27:8

"My heart has heard you say, 'Come and talk with me.'
and my heart responds, 'Lord I am coming.' "

✝ *13th February*

Whatever happens in your life will have to be borne. Your feelings of guilt are an extension of your sadness. They need to be addressed before you can come to terms with your grief. I am fully aware of your pain. The shock and incredible adjustment that you are experiencing is causing these feelings of distress.

Some of you are just beginning the journey, some are part-way and some are nearing its end. I am travelling with you. My empathy for your circumstances makes Me ever vigilant of your needs. I will continue to strengthen you through this trial. Have confidence that you will come out of it on the other side - a changed, stronger and more compassionate person. Trust that I am with you.

Ecclesiastes 3:4

"There is a time to cry and a time to laugh, a time to grieve and a time to dance."

✝ *14th February*

Don't allow your heart to be so downcast. Remember that nothing is for you to bear alone. I am always ready to comfort you. Close your eyes awhile and rest in My presence. The cry of your soul can be heard in heaven. I hear when you call and even though you may not be aware of it, I always respond.

Let Me tune your ears into My voice. This will be possible by your spending valuable time with me, by praying, reading My Word and listening in silence. There is much that I want to say to you, but I will not use force. If you feel alone today, remember that I am always with you. I feel joy in our intimate relationship. Put your hand in Mine and trust Me. I am love.

Proverbs 8:17-18

> *"I love all who love Me. Those who search for Me will surely find Me. Unending riches, honour, wealth and justice are mine to distribute."*

✝ *15th February*

Do you really know what I mean when I say "... *come to Me, all who are heavy laden and I will give you rest"?* I mean 'come and soak up My goodness with a thankful heart'. Meditate on My words, repeat them like a mantra. Tell me exactly how you feel, let your tears flow into My bottle and sit quietly in My presence and allow Me to speak.

Welcome My Spirit as I minister to your needs. Only 'I' can see into your soul, and only 'I' will not condemn what I find there. When you open yourself to My intimate scrutiny, it is then and only then that My real life-changing work will begin.

Prayer

Father, look into my exposed heart. Take my burdens from me and reveal Your hand at work. I am nothing without You. I want to let go of all of these troubles and relax with the certain knowledge that I am never alone. Amen.

✝ *16th February*

Tears are the physical release that you need; each tear will bring healing. Look around you and note that the world is also crying. I know that this doesn't aid your aching heart. In your agony, I want you to think of others. So many in this world are downhearted, I don't want My children to be so downcast that they become withdrawn.

If you feel inconsolable, you must seek out wise counsel. Never go a day without contact, not just with Me but also with someone else. Your heart will become barren if you give into this sorrow. No matter how dejected you feel I want you to share your feelings. Stay close to Me.

2 Corinthians 1:4

"He comforts us in all our troubles so that we can comfort others. When we are troubled, we will be able to give them the same comfort God has given us."

✝ *17th February*

Come to Me, My child, your anguish is distressing. Do not think that the sin of yesterday still separates us. I have forgiven you! You are washed clean by the blood of My Son. When will you realise and accept that His death and punishment were enough?

Your voice confesses something different to your mind. When Jesus hung on the cross, He said, "It is done!" Now believe that it is. I love you - why is that difficult for you to accept? My arms are waiting; come, My child, come.

2 Corinthians 5:18-19

"All this newness of life is from God, who brought us back to himself through what Christ did. And God has given us the task of reconciling people to him. For God was in Christ reconciling the world to himself, no longer counting people's sins against them."

✝ *18th February*

My Son suffered horrific things, and He did it gladly in love so that all My children would be free. The world talks about freedom of speech, but I have given you something greater - freedom of choice. Now go to My Word and read about My code for your daily lives. This will tell you the way I want you to live.

My Spirit will help you in wisdom, though the final decisions will be yours. My way gives you true freedom, you will understand this as you learn to penetrate My heart, when you read My Word.

Hebrews 4:12

"For the word of God is alive and active. Sharper than any double-edged sword, it penetrates even to dividing soul and spirit, joints and marrow; it judges the thoughts and attitudes of the heart."

✝ *19th February*

The winter months are the hardest because the season is barren and lifeless. But look for the beauty in these days. It's a time of rest for all that I created, including you. This exacting life has left you battered and bruised; just as the storms outside have destroyed the neatness of those pristine gardens.

Underneath new growth has already begun. Birds are busy attracting mates, and life below the surface is active. See the tiny snowdrops with their pure white bells, they don't shiver and hide. They give a promise of Spring, and their prominence is defiant against the sub-zero temperatures. I will strengthen you to be resilient. Get dressed in My love and show the world you are growing.

John 13:35

"Your love for one another will prove to the world that you are my disciples."

✝ *20th February*

Look at the glistening frost sparkling and thawing in the early morning sunshine. I will thaw the frosty shield you have built around your sadness. It's time for us to plan and prepare, I don't want you to remain in these dormant ways. I know you feel powerless to change your circumstances, but did the caterpillar expect to be a chrysalis forever?

When the time is right, he will develop into a beautiful butterfly, with bright, delicate wings. I will teach you to fly, but in order to fulfil My plans, I will need your co-operation. Place your hand in Mine, we are going on such a journey that you can't imagine. Trust Me.

1 Corinthians 1:9

"God will surely do this for you, for He always does
what He says, and He is the one who invited you into
this wonderful friendship with His Son, Jesus Christ our
Lord."

✝ *21st February*

When you look down into a frozen lake, the ice is hard and it splinters when broken. The top of the water freezes and protects the life underneath; air is trapped in order for the fish to survive; they slow their circulation to preserve energy. Do you see the similarities of your enclosed heart? Don't allow the frozen outer layers of your life to stop your search for Me. I don't want to be so deeply hidden in the centre that I can't get out.

I know that My children feel safe when they protect the interior from others, but trust that I have provided people with empathy. I use your life experiences to bless and serve others. Share your distress with a trusted friend, and I will infuse their advice with My wisdom.

Prayer

Father, help me to trust enough to share my feelings with someone trustworthy in confidence. Protect all I say in the love of a true friend. Thank you that you are leading me into opening up in my need and that kind words are your way of comforting me and showing that I am accepted, without judgement. In Jesus' name, Amen.

✝ *22nd February*

Close your eyes and imagine what is your dream? Tell Me about it. The dragonfly which hatches at the bottom of a muddy pond, has to put so much effort into achieving his freedom, that he almost exhausts himself. He struggles to climb up, to free himself from his circumstances. Imagine his joy when all his efforts are rewarded. He comes out of the water and faces a new life - freedom he had only dreamed about.

He dries his wings in the sun as soon as possible, then he's off, to a new exciting life of discovery. You can travel to freedom with Me, together we can enjoy the journey and focus on the goal. Surrender all in your life that holds you back – only you know what that is. My children are capable of so much, if only they would believe.

Job 11:13

> *"If only you would prepare your heart - lift up your hands in prayer! Get rid of your sins and leave all iniquity."*

✝ 23rd February

Can you feel the bright wintery sun warming your face? It is revitalising My creation. It will prompt some action in the ground, to start getting ready for Spring. During the dormant months, the earth took in nutrients from rotting vegetation. I have replenished it - ready for new growth.

My Word will consistently provide food for your lives, sustenance to live by. You will find all the nourishment you need to live a good, productive life in My teaching. Eat regularly, with a prayerful heart. If you are determined, then nothing can stop us from spending time together.

Psalm 107:9

"For he satisfies the thirsty and fills the hungry with good things."

✝ *24th February*

The early lambs are gambling in the fields! See the joy in their actions. Their lives are simple and unobstructed; all their concern is for feeding, playing and snuggling up to mum, for warmth. This is the kind of life I want My children to have, with the exception that you must also care for others. Don't over-complicate your lives.

If you put me at the centre, you will be fed; you will feel exuberant like the lambs, and My arms will always keep you warm. As I bless you, you in turn will want to bless others, and so the cycle of life will be maintained. Life will not always be smooth and without problems. I am your safety net, I will take care of you. Come to Me with your troubles and your joys!

1 Peter 2:9

> *"But you are not like that, for you are a chosen people. You are a kingdom of priests, God's holy nation, His very own possession. This is so you can show others the goodness of God, for He called you out of the darkness into His wonderful light."*

✝ *25th February*

I told you that My grace is sufficient for you. Do not add to your burdens by striving to always have them removed. I permit some things which will, in the long term, benefit you. Sometimes, My child, you need to recognise when the burden has already been removed and there is an element of your hanging on to it.

You feel safe in the familiar. Trust that, once given to Me, the matter is taken into My hands. Fret not, or else your burden will increase! I always have My eyes on you in case you begin slipping. Raise your eyes heavenward - I am here.

1 Peter 5:6-7

"Humble yourselves therefore under the mighty hand of God so that at the proper time he may exalt you, casting all your anxieties on him, because he cares for you."

✝ *26th February*

Appreciate the many blessings you have such as the joy of family. Savour each minute of your children growing up because the time passes so quickly. When you first looked down at that those tiny babies, such perfection of intricate detail, you couldn't have envisaged the people they would become, the paths they would take or the lives they would touch. Never stop steering them towards My Kingdom.

Power will be released in their lives by your constant prayer battle on their behalf. I will never let a child of Mine stray too far from Me and My purpose, without some intervention. I work consistently to keep them safe, to protect them from their disastrous decisions. When you bring your children to be christened, you are passing them into My protection. No matter where their road takes them, I will always be at the end of it.

Psalm 127:3

"Children are a gift from the Lord, they are a reward from him."

✝ 27th February

Everything I created is unique and important to Me. I want you to enjoy My creation, take time to look around you. Note the frosty spider's web blowing like lace in the breeze. Admire the glossy black bird, perkily hopping along, gorging on the bright winter berries. The thickness of the dark green hedge protects a multitude of living things in secret.

Examine the layers of productivity, each lending support to another life form, providing for each other, so that each species can survive. If My children would learn from their example, it would be a lesson in sharing. Each of you could manage happily on less and thereby free up some provision for someone else. No one should go hungry, no one should be without shelter; help each other by demonstrating My love.

Jeremiah 32:17

"Ah sovereign Lord you have made the heavens and the earth by your outstretched arm. Nothing is too hard for you."

✝ *28th February*

My creation has always recycled. You think it's a new invention. You have created this massive need to find use for things you have wasted. Packaging, chemicals that spoil the balance of nature, all are discarded. Commercialism has dictated to the consumer what they think they want.

Look at the natural development of things - nature recycles, it feeds, it restores, it replenishes. I want you to enjoy the modern world of technology, but not at the cost of damaging what should be simple. Progress getting out of hand breeds greed in My children. Guard your hearts and minds against materialism. I am all you need!

1 John 2:16-17

> *"For the world offers only the lust for physical pleasure, the lust for everything we see, and the pride in our possessions. These are not from the father, they are from this evil world. And this world is fading away along with everything it craves."*

✝ *29th February*

My precious child, your heart needs a rest. Your mind has been working around the clock in a turmoil of thoughts that are damaging you. Take time just to be. Enjoy your environment, devour some of the good things that I have given and just for a short time, consider your own need for refreshment!

There will be plenty of time to readjust back into the swing of things again. Let Me minister amidst the hurt and damage to your soul. Take My hand and let Me show you how to view your circumstances with a positive light. Things will not always be so extreme and harrowing.

Matthew 11:29-30

"Take my yoke upon you. Let me teach you because I am humble and gentle, and you will find rest for your souls, for my yoke fits perfectly and the burden I give you is light."

March

✝ 1st March

Very soon new life will uplift your mood and I want you to feel the excitement of change. Always I yield to My children's needs. I examine the position of your heart and I respond in My desire to encourage you. It will be the small delights that I leave for you along your path, that will bring your focus back to Me.

Examine the steps I lay out for you. Sometimes they are close together and will propel you with speed, but other times they are wider apart and you need to rest a while. Whatever distance is comfortable for you to travel, look to Me to equip you for the journey.

Judges 18:5-6

"Then they said, ask God whether or not the journey will be successful. Go in peace, the priest replied, for the Lord will go ahead of you on your journey."

✝ *2nd March*

Gather up the small treasures of encouragement that I offer you; as you travel with Me, you will see a use for them. I leave incentives that will add new meaning to your life. Use the many gifts you have been blessed with during your humble service to others.

Some of My children are more needy than you; I will put them across your path, so take care not to step over or go around them. Ask Me in what way I want their need to be met. Never tire of this mission - it will reward you as well as them. I see your heart and what I see pleases Me.

2 Thessalonians 3:13

"And I say to the rest of you brothers and sisters, never tire of doing good."

✝ 3rd March

The early bulbs have begun to poke shoots through the cold earth. Soon the garden will need your attention as the whole cycle of life begins. So too there is new growth within My children. I am doing many different things in your lives. I have spent the dormant winter months preparing. I work only at your speed, I plan, I nurture, I put new things in place, and this year I am planning a magnificent harvest.

Come let Me show you new things; listen carefully to My voice, and be willing and ready to react when I speak. Your salvation is completely assured, but I still want you to be proactive in this life. Love one another and My will, will be done.

2 Corinthians 9:10

"For God is the one who gives seed to the farmer and then bread to eat. In the same way he will give you many opportunities to do good; and he will produce a great harvest of generosity."

✝ 4th March

Leave your worries and look towards the horizon. Can you see the break in the clouds? Start to enjoy the palest of blue skies, I will make them aqua. Take time for yourself to appreciate the natural things around you, and be sensitive to the change in the season.

Your life is evolving, events will move you out of this dark path. Draw closer to Me, and I will direct when you are ready.

Prayer

> *Father, when I become insular in my own problems, thank*
> *You that you take time to show me a different life. Thank*
> *You that you don't leave me where I am and you only*
> *move me along in your perfect timing. Put me in pastures*
> *new and make me grow strong in you. Amen.*

✝ 5th March

There is an inerrant wind blowing; listen acutely for My leading and trust that what I say to you is true. Close your eyes, My child, and imagine your future with Me. Together we must work towards a new goal.

Your salvation is secure, bought at a very high price, but that doesn't mean you should drift through this life without having concern for others. Don't bury your talent whilst waiting for My Son to return for you. Use your gifts to serve Me and bless others.

1 Peter 4:10

"God has given gifts to each of you from his great variety of spiritual gifts. Manage them well so that God's generosity can flow through you."

✝ *6th March*

I am gathering My people. Spend time with Me and I will lift your spirits. Each of My children will feel the benefit of coming into communion with Me. It is good to start by opening My Word and then resting a while.

Tell Me of your immediate worries concerning yourself. Quietly wait for My answer. It may not come at once but learn to process when I speak into your mind - this will become easier with practice. Remember that what your consider good instinct is often My voice.

Hebrews 3:7

"That is why the Holy Spirit says, 'Today you must listen to him.'"

✝ 7th March

Tell Me of your anxieties for others by bringing them into My family. I am able to see not only your heart for them, but also their heart for you. Don't despair if they don't yet have a relationship with Me. Once you have shined My light upon them, I will never let it go out. Trust that I have these problems completely under My control.

I can bring about change in the darkest of situations. Look for the glimmer of hope that My light brings. Be patient, the flame will get stronger and in My timing there will be a huge floodlight that will enlighten your eyes to My purpose. Continue and be vigilant in your prayers for others.

Thought

Prayer is an ultimate relationship with God; it's asking for guidance and brings Him into the situations of others. Our Heavenly Father makes His own love and resources available to us if we ask Him.

✝ 8th March

It pleases Me to see the amazed gratitude of My children. It is then that I see the progress they are making. Rome truly wasn't built in a day, but it can be destroyed in an instant. That is how it is in your lives too. Sometimes you grow with slow repetition, going round and round as My people did in the desert. Other times you will see quick results. I use these times to encourage you.

In the days of what seems like little action, they will nevertheless teach and strengthen you. Welcome all seasons and continue to invite Me in to all areas of your life. I long for you to be aware of My presence.

Prayer

Father, forgive me when I don't notice your input in my life. Help me to be quick to learn and give me a new understanding of the way in which You teach me. I realise You allow some things for my good. Help me, when those times are painful, to accept and draw continually on Your strength. Amen.

✝ 9th March

There are many things I want to reveal to you - I will do this in many ways. Through your joy and sadness, through My creation, when you read My Word or listen to a sermon, through music, during prayer - these are just a few of the ways in which I communicate with you. Be assured that when you have a knowing in your heart - it is Me. I speak often in this way. Often My children still don't recognise My voice.

You have My Spirit living within you, and I want you to have confidence that you are hearing from Him. Some will call it a hunch; whatever name you give it, ask immediately if it's Me speaking. In time, with experience, you will 'just' know. I am all-powerful and My words are profound and will come into your mind from My gentle Spirit.

Prayer

Lord thank You for the variety of ways that You speak to me. Train me to know when it is Your voice that I am hearing. Our time together is unique and I appreciate all the different ways in which You communicate with me. Just as sheep know the shepherd's voice, help me to know Yours. Amen.

✝ *10th March*

Today I want you to examine the good things in your life and be thankful. Start from when you put your feet on the floor. Appreciate the comfort of your home and be grateful for your family. All My provision is for you, to make your life better. In the 'busyness' of your day, notice the things that I make available, things that you may take for granted. Imagine your life without these benefits.

Some of My children have none of these luxuries or amenities you take for granted. They have no extra clothing against the cold nights, no warm comfortable bed, no fresh water, let alone a flushing toilet, or a hot shower. Some don't know where their next meal will come from. Their children cry with the pain of hunger and disease. Can you feel their distress? Help them, My child! If you enjoy the benefits of My good things, show My love to those who don't.

2 Corinthians 8:8

> *"And God will generously provide all you need. Then you will always have everything you need and enough left over to share with others."*

✝ 11th March

Each one of My children is unique and has different ways of praising Me. I enjoy them all, from the flamboyant to the quietly grateful. Because you are different and do things in dissimilar ways, this does not mean that I enjoy one more than another. I want your worship to be comfortable and spontaneous.

It is something that is personal between the two of us and I relish the variation. All I ask is that you would do it with a smile in your hearts, and that your lips be sincere. Never feel pressured to behave as someone else does. My heart is gratified by your presence and that is sufficient for I see that your heart is rejoicing.

1 Chronicles 16:29

"Give to the Lord the glory he deserves. Bring your offering and come and worship him."

✝ *12th March*

Try not to look at the world with the eyes of the world. The inadequacies you see in yourself are not what I see when I look at you! You are made perfect in My Son. Jesus didn't die so that you would continue to find fault within yourselves. Learn to speak the truth that I see. If you believe Me, that you are made in My image, that the more time you spend with Me, the more like Jesus you become - then who can criticise?

Speak out the promises I have made to you, until you begin to live them. I recognise that there are things you have yet to understand, but enjoy My teaching and do not undervalue yourself. Be humble and modest but never self-deprecating.

Romans 12:2

"Don't copy the behaviour and customs of this world, but let God transform you into a new person by changing the way you think. Then you will know what God wants you to do, and you will know how pleasing and perfect His will is."

✝ *13th March*

My child, when I look at you, I see your goodness. I place thoughts deep within your heart to motivate you to share that goodness with others. Sometimes My children are able to quarry those feelings from within and use them to further My Kingdom. Never miss those opportunities which I continue to place on your path in numerous ways.

If you obey these feelings, there will always be a blessing at the conclusion. Be ever vigilant as you take advantage of these situations that make it possible for you to do something for someone else. I will bring favourable circumstances before you and encourage you to react with My love.

1 Thessalonians 3:12

"And may the Lord make your love grow and overflow to each other and to everyone else, just as our love overflows toward you."

✝ *14th March*

My Word is full of promises that I have made to you - over 5, 000. I am a faithful God and My unconditional love means that I will keep each one of My promises. Come to Me expectantly, and ready to receive in faith. There is so much that I want you to experience and faith is a key factor.

Open My Word, read My promises, speak them out loud into your life and above all, believe them! Never a second goes by when I am unaware of you - you can never hide from Me. Don't forget that I have cleansed you from your sin. There is a much better life available to you, take hold of My Word and believe it!

1 Corinthians 1:9

"No eye has seen, no ear has heard and no mind has imagined what God has prepared for those who love him."

✝ *15th March*

I enjoy your thankful heart. I love seeing you come to full realisation when you acknowledge My hand at work in your life. Draw strength from Me during those times; they were never meant to be unprofitable. Each event you encounter is another piece of your life's puzzle. Sometimes you assemble the part into the wrong place and then the scene is spoiled. I can quickly restore that which is good.

Trust that when you look back over life's trials, you will see that My love for you always overcame and always will, as long as you have a willing heart to follow Me. As you grow closer in fellowship with Me, you will learn to adapt and change direction when I speak. These times of uncertainty can cause you to be afraid, but put your hand in Mine and believe Me when I promise that I will never leave you.

Isaiah 41:13

"I am holding you by your right hand - I the Lord your God and I say to you, 'Do not be afraid. I am here to help you.'"

✝ *16th March*

Can you see the untamed power of the wind? It can pick up and move some tremendous weights and leave much destruction in its wake. It can bend the limbs and trunks of large trees even to the majestic oak - causing deformities; and yet, I can control this element. All that I have created will respond to My voice, yet I chose to give you free will. Use it wisely - you have a responsibility to future generations.

All that you do has a cause and effect, so be aware of the effect. I want you to seriously consider the results of your actions. Inconsiderate and uncaring attitudes are significant in affecting the ecological balance, which is causing so much destructive damage to the environment. You have a moral obligation to take care of the natural world that you live in. Time is shorter than you think.

Isaiah 24:5-6

"The earth suffers for the sins of its people, for they have twisted the instructions of God, violated his laws and broken his everlasting covenant. Therefore a curse consumes the earth and its people. They are left desolate, destroyed by fire. Few will be left alive."

✝ 17th March

Some of you will feel a sense of responsibility when you hear the reported damage to the environment. The problem is real and all of My children need to respond in a positive way. Without a combined agreement between all nations to halt the damage from progressing, it will not be enough. Fight for what you believe is right and necessary. Be constantly aware of wastage, especially wastage of clean water.

Some of My children who live in areas suffering from drought, are suffering dreadfully. It has a knock-on effect. Read the headlines, global warming is a very real problem. Future generations will have to deal with the effects, caused by this generation's selfish ignorance. Everyone must take a responsible role in this fight. Some irresponsible progress in this modern world has had an adverse effect. Listen to those who are trying to protect this planet.

Prayer

Father, forgive my apathy concerning the problems of this planet. Forgive my contribution towards its damage and make me question the waste, the pollution and all contributory factors that are within my capabilities to control. Forgive me for taking so much for granted and help me to become conscientious in the way I live. Amen.

✝ *18th March*

There are things that are coming to pass and I want you to be prepared for them. There are many prophesies in My Word; read them - from the Old Testament to the New. Don't be worried by what you discover, they will take place at the proper time. You are My children and I have promised I will never leave you, but you must get ready by studying My Word.

Learn of My promises and what the future holds for humanity, trust and do not be afraid. There will be a great movement amongst My people, but many more will be saved. Pay careful attention, be ever watchful, and allow My Spirit to lead you into the truth.

Matthew 24:14

"And the good news about the Kingdom, will be preached throughout the world, so that all nations will hear it; and then, finally the end will come."

✝ 19th March

My Son fought for and won your soul on the cross - why is it so hard for you to trust and believe? Would you contemplate dying such a death as His? His unconditional sacrifice must mean something to you? I long for you to surrender, all including the areas you feel inclined to hold back.

I will forgive every sin, and I understand that you are weak and will sin again, but your quick confession and remorse softens My heart. I will forgive the contrite heart and forget! Believe Me, My child, come to Me, repent and let My Spirit prepare you for the fight that is to come.

Matthew 24:9-13

"Then you will be arrested, persecuted and killed. You will be hated all over the world because of your allegiance to me. And many will turn away from me and betray and hate each other. And many false prophets will appear and will lead many people astray. Sin will be rampant everywhere and the love of many will grow cold. But those who endure to the end will be saved."

✝ *20th March*

Those of My children who are faithful will accept the truth. Hold onto this because My Spirit will open great revelations to you. Your part is to be obedient, vigilant, determined to have an intimate relationship with Me. I never force our intimacy, but equally I never forget when your heart cries out to Me.

I am ever watchful through your life's journey and I have never rushed you, but time is shortening. Ask My Spirit for clear understanding in your reasoning. I have a great desire to teach you, your part is to be willing to search.

Luke 11:9-10

"And so I tell you keep on asking and you will be given what you ask for. Keep on looking and you will find. Keep on knocking and the door will be opened. For everyone who asks, receives. Everyone who seeks, finds. And the door is opened to everyone who knocks."

✝ 21st March

I have complete power over darkness. If you come to Me, you will be in the light. Satan has no ability to influence you unless you give him permission. Call on My name when you are tempted, listen to the words of My Son.

For when Satan who is completely armed, guards his palace, it is safe - until someone who is stronger attacks and overpowers him, strips him of his weapons, and carries off his belongings.

Luke 11: 21-22

"For when Satan who is completely armed, guards his palace, it is safe - until someone who is stronger attacks and overpowers him, strips him of his weapons, and carries off his belongings."

✝ *22nd March*

Oh, My child, I know that you can hear Me, but you don't always act when I speak, this grieves My Spirit. Don't make any more excuses, spend time just sitting still with Me and take hold of the thoughts that come into your mind. Let go of past mistakes, and do not dwell on things that are forgiven. Do you want to continually punish yourself? What purpose can this serve?

Each time you store such a memory, you build a wall between us. Don't allow it to get so high that you can't see over it. Move on, My child, and release these negative thoughts of how bad you have been. You were bad when you were in darkness, but I have brought you into the light. By the blood of My Son, you are forgiven, washed clean, given a new life to begin again.

Colossians 1:21-22

"This includes you who were once far away from God. You were enemies, separated from him by your evil thoughts and actions. Yet now he has brought you back as his friends. He has done this by his death on the cross in his own human body. As a result he has brought you into the very presence of God, and you are holy and blameless as you stand before him without a single fault."

✝ *23rd March*

I want to transfer My thoughts into your thoughts. This will take much patience and practice from you. Come often into My presence, close your eyes and just tell Me you are ready. It will take time for our minds to become balanced but the sincere heart will have immense rewards. Each of you will find a different technique, learn to sharpen your senses until you become acutely aware of My Spirit.

Sometimes we will just sit quietly together, but as we perfect this special time, My words may be many. Be prepared to write down what I say. At other times, just rest with Me and allow Me in. Draw comfort from just being with Me. Our friendship will grow as we practice this closeness.

Revelation 3:20

"I stand at the door and knock, if you hear me calling and open the door I will come in and we will share a meal as friends. I will invite everyone who is victorious to sit with me on my throne, just as I was victorious and sat with My Father on his throne."

✝ 24th March

I have given My children different abilities. They are gifts to equip you in carrying out My work; it is up to you how you use these gifts. Because you are made in My image, you will have a desire to accomplish. Use these abilities wisely with a keen eye on the gospel teachings. These gifts will help to determine your quality of life; channel them towards good and use them to bless others.

Don't envy a gift I have given to someone else; look inside yourself to see what I have given to you. I want you to grow spiritually. Without My power, your talents are just dreams. I can help you fulfil potential. Pour out your grateful thanks for what I have given you and enjoy maximising your gifts as you use them for the benefit of My Kingdom.

Romans 12:6-8

"God has given each of us the ability to do certain things well, so if God has given you the ability to prophesy, speak out when you have faith that God is speaking through you. if your gift is that of serving others, serve them well. if you are a teacher, do a good job of teaching. if your gift is to encourage others, do it. If you have money share it generously. If God has given you leadership ability, take the responsibility seriously, and if you have a gift of showing kindness to others do it gladly."

✝ *25th March*

Can you sense how close I am, even during the times when you don't seem to need Me so much? I have not promised you a life free of problems but I have promised to help you through those times of strife, when you don't know which way to turn. But I want to share in your joy, so don't forget Me when things in your life are going well.

The angels sing when you have a thankful heart and the bad times recede into the background. You must still be on your guard during these days of happiness and do nothing that will give Satan a foothold. I love to see your laughter and the merriment in your eyes. Celebrate the good things that I provide in your life.

Psalm 16:11

"You will show me the way of life, granting me the joy of your presence and the pleasures of living with you forever."

✝ 26th March

Spring is just around the corner. Allow the new seeds that I am planting in your life to begin their journey. Each season is different and I love to see new growth in My children. Look around you for the changes that I am bringing about. During the dormant months, My hand is secretly at work. I never leave My children where I found them when they first invited Me into their lives.

I plan, I guide, I nurture, I will put you in contact with other Christians who will encourage you. If you haven't yet found a church family, I want you to look for one. It is important to fellowship with other Christians. If you are already established within a group, I want you to invest more time in learning from mature members of My body, and as you do so, I will oversee your growth.

Psalm 32:8

"The Lord says I will guide you along the best pathways for your life. I will advise you and watch over you."

✝ 27th March

My children, you are all different, your uniqueness sets you apart as you progress. Not all of you will fit into the establishment and that is fine, I accept and enjoy your differences. Search out what you are most suited to in My Kingdom. I love traditional worship and everything in between, up to and including the unconventional. I want you to feel comfortable when you come into My presence. Allow My Spirit to lead you. It doesn't matter to me in what way you worship, as long as you enjoy and seek fellowship with Me.

You have the freedom to discover what makes you happy during our time together - quiet contemplation or wild, head banging praise! It is what I see in your heart that is important. Come to Me often and we will share in a way that you feel the most comfortable and gives you the greatest joy.

Psalm 100:1-3

> *"Shout with joy to the Lord, O earth! Worship the Lord with gladness. Come before him singing with joy. Acknowledge that the Lord is God."*

✝ 28th March

Take time to enjoy the colours of the rainbow - it is there to remind you that I will never allow another flood to destroy that which I have built up. Do not be afraid that life's storms will overtake you. My peace will ensure that you are able to rest in the boat just as Jesus did.

Your faith pleases Me, so speak out this promise - 'You will keep in perfect peace all who trust in you, whose thoughts are fixed on you.' [Isaiah 26:3] No matter what happens in your life, trust that I am aware of it and I will act at the proper time.

Isaiah 26:7

"But for those who are righteous, the path is not steep and rough. You are a God of justice, and you smooth out the road ahead of them."

✝ 29th March

Find My peace amidst all the chaos; you can shelter in My unfailing love. You will find an inner stability with Me. This fallen world will always have turmoil, but you need never give in to it. No matter what is happening all around you, My peace will comfort you internally. Others will gaze in wonder as you remain calm during events that would cause them to crumble.

The inner light of My love will carry you as you trust that I am working diligently on your behalf. I will make you courageous - I will give you a greater source of strength than you ever imagined possible. I will remain close by to comfort and empower you to meet all adversity with peace and courage.

Isaiah 40:31

"But those who wait on the Lord will find new strength. They will fly high on wings like eagles. They will run and not grow weary. They will walk and not grow faint."

✝ *30th March*

Please grasp this truth - time is short! I will protect you from your enemies - not only physical enemies but everything that can separate you from Me. Drugs, alcohol, gambling, pornography, over-spending, under-giving - the list is endless. All that is hidden needs to come into the light. You may be unaware that these things come between us - they, if allowed, will become your gods.

'I am the Lord your God, you will have no other god but Me!' The closer you get to Me, the more Satan will try to intervene. I know that My children are under attack, I know the battles you have to fight. Let Me strengthen you. I am waiting to help you, but you must invite Me in and then be prepared to do what I ask. I will enable you to endure the pain.

Psalm 30:5

"His anger lasts for a moment but his favour lasts a lifetime. Weeping may go on all night, but joy comes in the morning."

✝ 31st March

Build one another up, consider what others are feeling and encourage them as a ready gift. Always look for the good in one another and in time the faults will go unnoticed. Treat one another with respect, consider their feelings before your own. Take Noah - in his obedience to Me, he suffered much from his critics. He was treated like a foolish man, but he remained faithful to My instructions.

Never judge others with harsh words when they appear to lack good sense. Practice kindness and be considerate; it is better to remain silent than to destroy someone's self-esteem. If Noah had caved in because he was laughed at, he and his family would have died. Don't allow your words to drown someone. Lift one another up, for each one of you is precious to Me.

Prayer

Father, help me always to treat others in the way I would hope they would treat me. Give me the gift of encouragement, never looking down on mistakes, but always praising their efforts. Discouragement serves no useful purpose and can easily destroy someone who is fragile. Make me sensitive and helpful in all I say and let me be a compassionate, shining light for You. Amen.

April

✝ *1st April*

My Son has sovereignty over the world. I recused Myself in order that the world would believe. If Jesus had ever sinned, there would be no redemption for sinners. Think of the enormity of the task He undertook. He did it willingly, but consider what He left behind in the light of what He came to do!

He humbled Himself and became a servant; He was born in the poorest of circumstances. As a tiny baby, His life was threatened, so His earthly parents protected Him and they became refugees when there was a distinct lack of law and order and life was cheap. He entered the world knowing full well what life had in store for Him. Believe Me when I tell you that His unconditional sacrifice will save all those of you who believe in Him.

John 14:6

"I am the way the truth and the life. No one can come to the father except through me. If you had known who I am, then you would have known who my father is. From now on you know him and have seen him."

✝ 2nd April

My Son's covenant to save the world began on the day Adam and Eve first sinned. You must first acknowledge what My Son did and then by My grace, come to Him in grateful acceptance. I want you to fully comprehend that Jesus died for you, in order to prevent you and Me being eternally separated.

I cannot look upon sin. Jesus is in My presence continually pleading on your behalf. I do not judge you because you are made righteous by His blood and you belong to Him.

Hebrews 9:15

> *"That is why he is the one who mediates the new covenant between God and people, so that all who are invited can receive the eternal inheritance God has promised them. For Christ died to set them free from the penalty of the sins they had committed under that first covenant."*

✝ *3rd April*

My Son is the foundation of all truth. He came to you and lived as a man, but He was never a separate entity from Me. He is the source of eternal life. Do not allow yourselves to be deceived. He is all that is good and steadfast and without Him, you could not come into My presence.

The Word is a standard of holiness; My Son is the living concept of holiness. Remember to begin each day with confession and thankfulness, then believe you are forgiven and even the stain of sin is removed. How then can I remember your sins when you are washed clean by the blood of My son? You are loved beyond anything you could imagine.

John 1:1-4

> *"In the beginning the word already existed. He was with God, and he was God. He created everything there is. Nothing exists that he didn't make. Life itself was in him, and this life gives life to everyone."*

✝ *4th April*

Don't let your experience in adversity cause a separation between us. With My help and guidance, the difficulties you face will make you stronger. Trust Me that although I know about each distressing one, you must still invite Me into them. It is My longing to share every part of your life.

The angels, just like you, are My servants and will do My bidding. I dispatch them to intervene on your behalf, only when there is a need. The eventualities in your life would be much easier for you if you learned to have complete trust in Me. Look up these scriptures and be encouraged as you read them prayerfully:

Genesis 6:5-22, 1 Peter 1:8, 1 Corinthians 1:9, Jonah 2:2, Habakkuk 3:19, Isaiah 26:3.

1 Peter 1:9

"Your reward for trusting him will be the salvation of your souls."

✝ 5th April

There is much in the spiritual realm that remains a mystery. If you trust Me I will reveal things to you when the time is right. It delights Me when My children trust Me without first understanding. I accept though that some of you have analytical minds. You are 'born again' as little children which means you accept without question right from the beginning. I will then teach you by many methods, at your own pace.

This teaching, however, requires you to have a very real involvement. A very real thirst for knowledge and a yearning to know Me. Again, the best source of explanation is My Word. Wherever you are in your walk with Me, you must come prayerfully, expectantly, and with an open mind; then the secrets hidden in My Word can be revealed to you.

Prayer

Father, thank you for the availability of so many resources to help me build up my relationship with You. I humbly believe and want to learn more. Open new revelations as I study and pray, always allowing time for You to speak. I welcome You into my life; thank you for encouraging me.

Amen.

✝ *6th April*

I want each of you to listen to My voice. I am everywhere and you need to recognise that I am training you. It is important that you become aware of the gifts I have blessed you with. I have anointed each of My children, and I want you to use your talents to further My Kingdom here on earth.

When you discover that you are good at something, no matter what it is, such as mopping floors, remember - it is a gift. Do it for Me. In each action, whisper My name - I will hear you. Humble beginnings, done with reverence, pave the way for promotion. I will make all your offerings shine.

Proverbs 8:6

> *"Listen to me for I have excellent things to tell you.*
> *Everything I say is right. For I speak the truth and hate*
> *every kind of deception. My advice is wholesome and good.*
> *There is nothing crooked or twisted in it. My words are*
> *plain to anyone with understanding, clear to those who*
> *want to learn."*

✝ 7th April

Take time to enjoy My world. Don't feel guilty about the good things you have. When you look around, My gifts may seem unequally divided. Sometimes if you think that others haven't got as much as you, do not worry. Their needs are ever of concern to Me.

If you have a compassionate heart and are aware of the needs of others, it is My Spirit which is leading you. Take action to help them. You are My hands and people will see Me in what you do for them. I despise all the misery that the 'prince of darkness' heaps upon My children. Fight the darkness in this world by using My light.

Galatians 6:10

"Whenever we have the opportunity, we should do good to everyone, especially to our Christian brothers and sisters."

How blessed to know a person who is as beautiful inside as well as the outside. The world trains its eyes to appreciate outward appearances, but I look deeper. Your heart and subsequent actions are what is important to Me. I made you all and you are all special.

✝ 8th April

How blessed to know a person who is as beautiful on the inside as on the outside. The world trains its eyes to appreciate outward appearances, but I look deeper. Your heart and subsequent actions are what are important to Me. I made you all and you are all special.

In time, the true essence of beauty will be revealed and will be rewarded. Inner beauty prevails and grows into something magnificent. Age will cause outward beauty to fade; the light that glistens from within, brightens everything it touches. Reach out to one another in My perfect love.

1 Samuel 16:7

"But the Lord said to Samuel, 'Don't judge by his appearance or height, for I have rejected him.' The Lord doesn't make decisions the way you do! People judge by outward appearance, but the Lord looks at a person's thoughts and intention

✝ 9th April

Tell Me what you need that you feel you lack. I am asking what you need not what you want. Sometimes the two are combined, but often they are separate. I long to give you good things and address your needs, both immediate and long term. The joy I get from blessing you is boundless, especially when you appreciate what you already have.

I refer now to the spiritual gifts that will help you to grow in Me. Look out for the little changes, the small steps of progress and affirmation from others that indicate something excellent in you. My desire is that you improve these talents and utilise them for the benefit of others. Ask Me to show you what areas of your life I want to develop.

Psalm 32:8

"The Lord says I will guide you along the best pathway of your life."

✝ *10th April*

Start each day by asking Me to rebuke Satan on your behalf with the words - "the Lord rebuke you".[Jude 9] The more intimate our friendship, the more frequently you will come under attack from the powers of darkness. These attacks are very real and will take on many disguises. Only by putting on your spiritual armour and speaking My Name into every situation, will you be safe.

The ways of darkness can be very subtle and whisper into your weakness. Jesus fought for you to overcome and He still fights. A time is coming when there will be much more deception in this world. Make a daily stance against the 'prince of darkness'. I will empower you to resist him. You must be ready and willing to act and claim the promises of My Word.

Ephesians 6:14-18

"Stand your ground by putting on the sturdy belt of truth and the body armour of God's righteousness. For shoes put on the peace that comes from the good news, so that you will be fully prepared. In every battle you will need faith as your shield, to stop the fiery arrows aimed at you by Satan. Put on salvation as your helmet, and take the sword of the spirit, which is the word of God. Pray at all times on every occasion in the power of the Holy Spirit."

✝ *11th April*

Have you ever watched the speed and strength of a tiny ant? It can lift up to 50 times its own body weight and run about 300 metres an hour. It protects aphids in order to have a food supply. It has two stomachs: one for itself and one designed to hold food for other ants. Look how intricately I have made them.

How much more complex are you, My child! Your body can accomplish great feats but it is the mind that is the most intricate. It needs the rest of the body to maintain a healthy function, and it takes 20% of the oxygen you breathe to keep your brain tissues alive. As My body, the Church needs every member. I want you to experience unity.

1 Corinthians 1:10

"Now dear brothers and sisters, I appeal to you by the authority of the Lord Jesus Christ to stop arguing among yourselves. Let there be real harmony so there won't be divisions in the church. I plead with you to be of one mind, united in thought and purpose."

✝ 12th April

I have placed many fruits of the Spirit within you. Use what My son died for you to have. You have opportunities to develop these qualities, and I will help you. All the spiritual seeds that I have planted are to make you a better person, and by your faith you will gradually change into the likeness of My Son.

Believe that these fruits are already within your heart, draw on My strength and be assured that the roots are secure. Day by day, with your constant determination, I will water your faith and the fruits that you display will confirm that you are My child.

Galatians 5:22

"But when the Holy Spirit controls our lives he will produce this kind of fruit in us; love, peace, patience, kindness, goodness, faithfulness, gentleness and self-control."

✝ *13th April*

You and I are on this journey together. Trust that I know what the future holds. I know how you will react to each new challenge and I will equip you to face each one. Be determined to follow Me and be obedient to My teaching.

When things don't go the way you have planned, have faith that they are only minor setbacks that I have within My control. Don't allow darkness to dull your vision. The vision is a seed from Me. Take every opportunity as a learning curve. Your faith will grow as we conquer things together.

James 1:3-4

"For when your faith is tested, your endurance has a chance to grow. So let it grow, for when your endurance is fully developed, you will be strong in character and ready for anything."

✝ *14th April*

Come to Me and ask for healing. This is an area that many of My children avoid, and their lack of faith can hold back My blessings. Sometimes you are wounded as a result of sin and although I have forgiven you, the damage lingers on. My power can be more easily demonstrated in your weakness. This means that some of you are able to serve Me more effectively, even before you are made whole.

Your faith must be developed to receive My healing. This isn't to say that I won't heal someone who has little faith, but you must learn to accept that I can see the bigger picture and My timing is perfect. Others may be blessed through your weakness. To receive healing from sin, you need to be made right with Jesus.

Psalm 119:93

"I will never forget your commandments; for you have used them to restore my joy and my health."

✝ 15th April

My child, stop rushing the things that are important. It is very easy for you to get side-tracked and thereby end up on the wrong route. Again, you need to have faith. I will make you sure-footed but you must spend time with Me. I want you to have victory in this life. All those who are successful in their field must train and practise their skill.

It is so in your decision to follow Me; unless you get to know My heart you will be unable to progress. The more time you spend studying My Word, opening your life to Me, the closer we will become. I know you inside out and I love you; I want you to be the same with Me.

1 Corinthians 9:24-25

"Remember that in a race everyone runs, but only one person gets the prize. You must run in such a way that you will win. All athletes practice strict self control. They do it to win a prize that will fade away, but we do it for an eternal prize."

✝ *16th April*

I know that your earthly bodies are ageing. The aches and pains you suffer remind you of your fragility. But, those of you who are My children, can look forward with confidence to the day you will receive a heavenly body.

It will be a body that will be free from sickness and disease, a body fit for eternal life without fatigue or limitations. My Son is resurrected and is no longer bound by earthly restrictions. Those of you who believe in Him will also be resurrected to eternal life.

1 Corinthians 15:42-44

"It is the same way for the resurrection of the dead. Our earthly bodies, which die and decay, will be different when they are resurrected, for they will never die. Our bodies now disappoint us, but when they are raised they will be full of glory. They are weak now but when they are raised they will be full of power. They are natural human bodies now, but when they are raise, they will be spiritual bodies."

✝ *17th April*

Never be proud of your purity and use it to be superior over others. I love all My children equally. You are all at different stages in your commitment to Me and just because some of you know Me better, doesn't mean that you are superior. Take time to help each other grow without condemnation.

The road is a long one and will become narrower the further down it you go. Have patience and understanding with each other. Sometimes, I put your hand in another's, just as My hand is in yours. You are My Church - My Body. When you work together in harmony, great things can be accomplished. This pleases Me.

1 Corinthians 2:5-8

"I am not overstating it when I say that the man who caused all the trouble, hurt your entire church, more that he hurt me. He was punished enough when most of you were united against him. Now it is time to forgive him and comfort him. Otherwise he may become so discouraged, that he won't be able to recover. Now show him that you still love him."

✝ *18th April*

Don't put things off, My child. I know that you easily get distracted with worldly things. If you delay what you should have done today, then tomorrow may be too late and another opportunity may not arise.

My children have a basic desire to do good, but tend to listen to that whispering voice that says someone else will do it. I have equipped you with the capacity to have a deep love for one another. Jesus left you with that commandment, so put others needs before your own. Do it now, My child.

Proverbs 3:26-28

> *"For the Lord is your security, he will keep your foot from being caught in a trap. Do not withhold good from those who deserve it, when it is in your power to help them. If you can help your neighbour now, don't say, "come back tomorrow and then I will help you."*

✝ 19th April

Make sure you offer security to your children, just as I offer security to Mine. I know only too well how hard it is with a rebellious child. Patience and love will win in the end. Children will honour and respect their parents when they are secure in the necessary ground rules. Train your children early and be firm in your guidance.

Be honest and consistent, only backing down if you are at fault or being too harsh. Use My Word for a model for your parenting skills. In morality, teach your children right from wrong. When they are christened in My name, I will never let them go.

Ephesians 6:4

"And now a word to you fathers, don't make your children angry by the way you treat them. Rather bring them up with discipline and instruction approved by the Lord."

✝ *20th April*

You must accept whatever situation I have put you in. If you are blessed with a Christian marriage, you must keep My commandments concerning sexual intimacy. If you are a lone Christian in your marriage, you must pray diligently for your spouse and look for blessings in your marriage.

Always be aware of your Christian duty, putting love above all else. Be kind and faithful, never allowing the sun to go down on your grievances towards each other. Be the first to apologise regardless of fault and continually invite Me into your relationship.

1 Corinthians 7:14

> *"For the Christian wife brings holiness into her marriage, and the Christian husband brings holiness into his marriage."*

✝ *21st April*

I expect that sometimes you will get bored. Repetitive things that seem to have no worthwhile result can weary you. Some of My children find it difficult to say 'no', when asked to do something they would really rather not. A sense of duty is admirable, but can be misplaced. Listen to My voice so you really will know when it's Me who is asking you. Your spirit will be excited.

If you are completing a task with My blessing, you will have a joyful spirit, the necessary ability and equipment. Take heart, My child, there are many talents available for each task. I will give you enthusiasm to accomplish whatever I ask of you.

Galatians 5:25

"If we are living now by the Holy Spirit, let us follow the Holy Spirits leading in every part of our lives."

✝ *22nd April*

Rest in Me and you will learn to be content in every situation. Material wealth will not satisfy you and bring you fulfilment. You are well off, My child, when your prayers bring you peace, because then you are trusting that I will take care of things. Your joy comes from a relationship with Me.

Your faith is increased by allowing Me to share in your life and as you come to an increasing realisation of My love. This life is only temporary and each of your burdens will be bearable when you are yoked to Me. I have already given you peace, accept it and draw strength from Me, as you face each obstacle.

Philippians 4:11-13

"Not that I was ever in need, for I have learned to get along happily, whether I have much or little. I have learned to live on almost nothing or with everything. I have learned the secret of living in every situation, whether it's with a full stomach or empty, with plenty or little. For I can do everything with Christ who gives me the strength I need."

✝ *23rd April*

I love all of you equally, no matter what race you are. There has been racism throughout history, it is not a modern invention. No one has the right to judge others, least of all because of their ethnicity. I have made you all in My image.

Shame on those who despise the colour of someone's skin! Shame on those who despise someone because of their accent, or where they come from! Shame on your prejudice against your neighbour! I love every race and culture, and I want all of My children to feel the same.

Colossians 3:11

> *"In this new life it doesn't matter if you are a Jew or a Gentile, circumcised or uncircumcised, barbaric, uncivilised, slave or free. Christ is all that matters and he lives in all of us."*

✝ 24th April

My children, you pray fervently when you want something and I long to answer in a positive way, but how often do you remember to thank Me? If you gave someone a present and they snatched it from you without any appreciation, how would that make you feel? Your needs are always My concern, but if you have an ungrateful attitude, it saddens Me.

I love to hear how much better your life is when I have answered your prayer. Our relationship is a two-way partnership. I want to hear about the good times you experience as well as the bad. Come to Me always with a thankful heart - it will play a huge role in the maturing of your faith.

Colossians 4:2

"Devote yourself to prayer with an alert mind and a thankful heart."

✝ 25th April

Don't ignore your conscience - that is the Holy Spirit speaking to you. When you belong to Me, you will hear His voice, prodding you with uncomfortable feelings when you sin. The natural response you will feel will be shame; you may blush and feel guilt, and you will want forgiveness and reconciliation.

Don't evade Me when this happens. Come quickly and confess, and I will immediately forgive you. Sin will have some consequences - not necessarily exposure, but you may have mental anguish or physical repercussions. Sin always causes pain to someone, but I will show you how to overcome.

Ezra 9:6

"I prayed, 'O my God, I am utterly ashamed; I blush to lift up my face to you. For our sins are piled higher than our heads, and our guilt has reached to the heavens.'"

✝ *26th April*

When I call upon you to do a job for Me, I call upon all of your abilities. I will equip you, but you must be prepared to put in some planning, preparation and perseverance. The rewards will be a real blessing to you. Don't be afraid of being inadequate, if I have given you a task, we will see it through together.

I will ensure that you grow in the areas most needed and if you feel that you are struggling, I will give you encouragement. Go ahead with vigour and fortitude. Do not look too closely at obstacles, there will always be setbacks from outside quarters, this is part of life, They will not prevail against the two of us, I will provide all that you need.

Prayer

Lord, show me a vision for my life and provide me with the means to realise it. It is my privilege to accomplish things for You. I don't want my fear of inadequacy to prevent my achieving the goal You have set for me. Thank You for your gifts that will enable me to carry out Your purpose. In Jesus name, Amen.

✝ *27th April*

When you pray for that which pleases Me and lines up with My will, you can pray with confidence. Don't treat your prayers as a magic formula to get exactly what you want. I love to hear from you and I know what you want before you ask, but don't let that stop you from consulting Me. Remember, when I say no, it could mean - not yet. I may have something better for you; giving you an answer in the affirmative could do you more harm than good.

Don't pout like a spoiled child if you don't get what you want, but trust Me that I really do have something which is superior planned. Your prayer life is an important part of our friendship; as you communicate with Me, we will grow closer. I love to hear from you, but please don't make your prayers just a shopping list of requests. Rather, speak to me sometimes just because you want to.

1 John 5:14-15

"And we can be confident that he will listen to us whenever we ask for anything in line with his will. And if we know he is listening when we make our requests, we can be sure he will give us what we ask for."

✝ *28th April*

Selfishness inhibits My love in your life. The sins of this world are deeply embedded in your hearts and you must fight these powers of darkness every day. Numerous occasions present themselves for you to help someone else by responding in a positive way and these responses will become second nature to you.

Give of yourself wherever there is a need. Your kindness can go a long way when I bless it and the seed grows. Give of your money without worrying if you will have sufficient left. I will replenish and even multiply your generosity. Let the world see that you are My child by the deeds that you do.

1 John 3:17

"But if anyone has enough money to live well and sees a brother or sister in need and refuses to help - how can God's love be in that person?"

✝ 29th April

Be on your guard against errant teaching. Just because someone teaches in My Name, doesn't mean that it will always be biblical truth. Don't compromise on something that is incorrect. Be very careful how you evaluate My Word - some teaching is mistaken, some is deliberate. Only by your searching of the scriptures, can you be sure.

Compromise can slip into other parts of your life and you could inadvertently begin to sin, by being lax about My commandments. It is always easier not to rock the boat and think that if society deems something acceptable, who are you to argue. You are My child and must stand up for My Word.

2 John 1:9

"For if you wander beyond the teaching of Christ, you will not have fellowship with God. But if you continue in the teaching of Christ, you will have fellowship with both the father and the son."

✝ 30th April

Creation has been a subject of intrigue for man over the centuries. Man makes it too complicated by his scientific research. Yes, science has its place, but My Word puts creation very simply and honestly in these words – "In the beginning God created ..."

The world and all that's in it, is so complex in its design and function, that it did not, and could not, have occurred by accident! It was designed and created by My hand and My hand alone. I have complete power over the universe and all that is in it.

Genesis 2:1-3

> *"So the creation of the heavens and the earth and everything in them was completed. On the seventh day, having finished his task, God rested from all his work. And God blessed the seventh day and declared it holy, because it was the day when he rested from the work of creation."*

May

 1st May

This world is full of temptations - things that are painted in a deceptive way to make them appear normal and attractive. I know the constant battles you have, My child. A battle is being waged for your soul, by the presentation of things which are just a little bit wrong. Satan used an inoffensive apple to tempt Eve. It devastated My plan by allowing sin to enter the world.

The 'prince of darkness' knows your weaknesses, just as you do. Take care not to be exposed in those weak places. Turn away before temptation becomes an issue. Pray for protection of your soul as you cling to My will.

Matthew 18:8

"So if your hand or foot causes you to sin, cut it off and throw it away. It is better to enter heaven crippled or lame than to be thrown into the unquenchable fire with both your hands and feet."

✝ 2nd May

Don't blame others for your iniquities. Take responsibility for your own mistakes and confess them to Me. I will forgive you, My child; by the blood of Jesus, you are fully redeemed. Modern society has slipped fully into the blame game. Adam blamed Eve, who in turn blamed satan. When My children have done something wrong, I can see that My Spirit which is present within them, causes them to squirm.

Your heart will be heavy if you persist in hanging onto your sin. Be wary that one wrong action can so readily lead to another. Don't bury yourselves in a pit of dishonesty. Conform to My commandments and the world will acknowledge that you are different, because you belong to Me.

Genesis 3:12

> *"Yes Adam admitted, 'but it was the woman you gave me who brought me the fruit and I ate it.' Then the Lord God asked the woman, 'How could you do such a thing?' 'The serpent tricked me,' she replied, 'that's why I ate it.'*
> "

✝ 3rd May

When you have union as husband and wife, you become one. This relationship is a blessing and I want it to give you joy. This act should not be done indiscriminately, without feeling any commitment to each other. It is an act of intimacy, by a physical joining of two souls, and it can expose a unique vulnerability in each party.

Consider your partner and do not take each other for granted. Protect this act of joining together as sacred. Resist giving in to temptation or participating in fleeting affairs. Guard your sexual desire from taking forbidden fruit. When you are faithful to your spouse and you love each other, I will bless your relationship.

1 Corinthians 7:3-4

> *"The husband should not deprive his wife of sexual intimacy which is her right as a married woman, nor should the wife deprive her husband. The wife gives authority over her body to her husband and the husband gives authority over his body to his wife."*

✝ 4th May

Do not rush too quickly into relationships that could in the long-term damage your relationship with Me. I have taught you the basic truth of what is an acceptable friendship and what you should have nothing to do with. Your free will sometimes interferes with your common sense and you end up in an ill-advised relationship.

If you come hastily to Me, My Spirit will guide you. Don't ignore His leading. I see the longing of your heart and I can change all situations. Don't allow your feelings to overcome what you know to be the truth of My Word. I want to protect you, but in order for you to become wise, there are certain situations that I will permit. It pleases Me when you request My guidance. Listen for that inner voice and do not be dissuaded by others.

Prayer

*When my need for a special relationship becomes too
important to me, help me to take time to re-evaluate.
When I seek Your discernment, open my eyes to accept it.
Give me clear interpretation of Your Word and protect my
lonely heart from making mistakes. Amen.*

✝ 5th May

You have an endless ability to deceive yourself. My protection is offered to you daily but you must take heed of My words. I know the deepest secrets of your heart, and I cry with you when you hurt. It does not need to be this way. If you would seek My face early each day, with anticipation of My guidance - the path would not be so arduous.

Open your mind to your self-deceptions; this will become a skill in time. I know that this deceit is not intentional and it takes many forms. Do not convince yourself of the rightness of something just because you want it to be so.

1 Corinthians 4:4-5

"My conscience is clear, but that isn't what matters. It is the Lord himself who will examine me and decide. So be careful not to jump to conclusions before the Lord returns as to whether or not the Lord is faithful. When the Lord comes he will bring our deepest secrets to light and will reveal our private motives. And then God will give to everyone whatever praise is due."

✝ 6th May

Turn to Me, My child, when you need comfort. When you were a little one, you turned to your parents at such times. You are My little one and My arms are ever open wide and welcoming. Nothing that you have done or gone through is beyond My love for you. I understand all the deepest hurts in your life.

I long to wipe away your tears, to remove your distress and to let you melt into the gentleness of My love. Tell Me about all of your disappointments, your fear and pain. Come instinctively to Me and I will cleanse you inside your heart, just as a mother cleans the cut on her child's knee.

2 Thessalonians 2:16-17

"May the Lord Jesus Christ and God our Father, who loved us and in his special favour gave us everlasting comfort and good hope, comfort your hearts and give you strength in every good thing you do and say."

✝ 7th May

My child, you have got so caught up in your life that other matters have taken priority over Me and our time together is being neglected. I know that this is not a deliberate act but you need to guard against our lost time. It will be so easy for us to become estranged. I miss you and I wait in the background for you to remember Me.

Church meetings and biblical courses are good, but should not take precedence over our quality time together. Leaders of the church should ask for My help in better managing their time. I know that your heart misses Me, in the same way that I miss you.

Revelation 2:5

> *"Look how far you have fallen from your first love! Turn back to me again and work as you did at first! If you don't I will come and remove your lamp stand from its place among the churches."*

✝ *8th May*

Have you lost your enthusiasm for My Word, the church, or Me? Pray aggressively that I will revive you. Spiritual attacks are ever-present, seeking to engineer your downfall. If all that I once meant to you has become dull and your sensitivity to holiness has become mundane and joyless, you must seek help from your spiritual leaders.

Tell Me what has led to your feeling drained in My presence? I know that these feelings are tangible in your life, but you and I can get to the root cause of this decay. In faith, confess the way you feel, open your heart fully and show Me the true state of your soul.

Romans 8:26-28

"And the Holy Spirit helps us in our distress. For we don't even know what we should pray for, nor how we should pray. But the Holy Spirit prays for us with groaning that cannot be expressed in words. And the father who knows all hearts knows what the spirit is saying, for the spirit pleads for us believers in harmony with God's own will."

✝ *9th May*

Even when you don't make the best decisions, I will still work them out for good, both in your life and those around you who are also affected. The prevalence for evil in this fallen world can, by your susceptible emotions, interfere with that which I had planned. I want you to be happy but not at the cost of My purpose.

There may be consequences of your poor choices, but never despair. Come to Me with hope and a contrite heart. That which was haunting you is a mistake that I will use for your benefit and the good of those around you. Having free will often undermines your decision-making. My input later on will avert disaster.

Proverbs 2:7

"He grants a treasure of good sense to the Godly. He is the shield, protecting those who walk with integrity. He guards the paths of justice and protects those who are faithful to him."

✝ *10th May*

My child, commit to a serious study of My Word and then apply what you learn to your everyday life. Focus systematically on hearing from Me through all that I teach you. When I can see you are intent on opening the mysteries of the Bible, I will bless you with wisdom.

Verses that you have read many times will suddenly have new meaning for you. I will bless you with an excited discernment as you search the Scriptures. You will discover my heart inside the pages. Let this be a new venture that you will undertake with My guidance. My Spirit will lift you to new heights.

Proverbs 4:1

> *"My children, 'Listen to me. Listen to your father's instruction, pay attention and grow wise. For I am giving you good guidance. Don't turn away from my teaching.' "*

✝ *11th May*

My child, yield your thoughts to My input. Accept My peace even though your heart is in turmoil. Draw on the things of Me that you may not yet understand, the concept of which, in time, will become clear. Be satisfied with knowing only as much as I reveal, until you are ready to understand more.

Take all that I offer with thanksgiving in your heart. When I see that you are capable of handling more, I will enlighten your mind. Accept all that I have blessed you with and cheerfully use it for the benefit of others. I will watch you closely even though I may be silent for a while.

Hebrews 10:23-24

"Without wavering, let us hold tightly to the hope we say we have, for God can be trusted to keep his promise. Think of ways to encourage one another to outbursts of love and good deeds."

✝ *12th May*

I want you to revel in the experience of belonging to Me. You are secure, nothing in the world can separate you from My love. Nothing you do could make Me love you more - or less. My blessings are rich and satisfying. I accept you! Accept My love with awe and great joy.

Don't take our relationship for granted; rather be obedient and submissive. There will be power released in our togetherness. Don't leave Me on the outside; allow me to share in your life so that you can feel the contentment and satisfaction of being My precious child.

Deuteronomy 28:9-10

"If you obey the commands of the Lord your God and walk in his ways, the Lord will establish you as his holy people, as he solemnly promised to do. Then all the nations of the world will see that you are a people claimed by the Lord and they will stand in awe of you."

✝ *13th May*

Your senses have the capacity to become acutely aware of spiritual things. Each day you see miracles occurring in My world - new life beginning, changing seasons, your body healing itself. All these things happen so frequently that you take them for granted.

I am the architect of the world and am all around you in everything you see. Believe in My Son; just as I raised Him from the dead, My promise is that I will resurrect you! I want you to have the good life that He died for you to have. Become one with Me, and allow your spirit the freedom to join with Me.

Hebrews 2:4

"And God verified the message by signs and wonders and various miracles and by giving gifts of the Holy Spirit whenever he chose to do so."

✝ *14th May*

The seeds that I planted in you before you were born, have been growing throughout your life. All of you shine individually. If a sense of significance still eludes you, listen to your friends when they pay you compliments. Have the boldness to test the waters. When I have blessed you with a gift, I will also bless you to become excellent.

I want My children to be humble, but that doesn't mean you should ignore that inner voice which speaks the truth of encouragement when you are capable of something. The task will be easy for you because of My blessing. My power will cause you to achieve and expand your horizons.

Romans 4:20-22

> *"Abraham never wavered in believing God's promise. In fact his faith grew stronger and in this he brought glory to God. He was absolutely convinced that God was able to do anything he promised. And because of Abraham's faith God declared him righteous."*

✝ *15th May*

I love to see your heart melt with compassion, when you come across another person in pain. Step up your prayers for it places Me in the centre of their problem. Nothing you ever say to Me goes unnoticed. As I feel your heart become heavy with the traumatic events of this cruel world, My angels are released to rush to the side of those in need.

I motivate those in a position to involve themselves in the circumstances of another. You, My child, are included from both aspects. Never allow the fear that situations will remain the same, to prevent you from jumping to the aid of someone who needs help; or accepting help in your own circumstances, when they seem impossible to change. My hand is always available to you.

2 Corinthians 1:4

> *"He comforts us in all our troubles so that we can comfort others. When others are troubled we will be able to give them the same comfort God has given us."*

✝ *16th May*

Many times, My child, I will bring you into relationships that will give you a mutual bond. Empathy is a very moving emotion and when two people have been through similar experiences, it enables them to help each other. Never shy away from your own pain, or that which belongs to someone else.

Sharing a story with a trusted friend can bring much comfort to both parties and a renewed closeness. Look for My hand at work as I weave together the fine threads of your life into the rich tapestry of others. Friendships are born in this way - with mutual understanding.

2 Corinthians 1:6-7

"So when we are weighed down with troubles, it is for your benefit and salvation! For when God comforts us, it is so that we in turn, can be an encouragement to you. Then you can patiently endure the things we suffer. We are confident that as you share in suffering, you will also share God's comfort."

✝ *17th May*

Your conscience, My child, is born of My Spirit correcting your wrong thinking or wrong actions. My Spirit prompts you when you stray from My laws. Your conscience can revisit indiscretions long after they are forgiven and forgotten; you may burn with shame when you recall them.

It will be to your advantage to accept My forgiveness and forget the sin. Who are you then to remember and refuse to forgive yourself? Take it to heart that when you have been forgiven, you must let it rest. Put on your spiritual armour against the temptations of the devil.

1 Timothy 11:19-20

"Cling tightly to your faith in Christ and always keep your conscience clear for some people have deliberately violated their consciences, as a result their faith has been ship wrecked."

✝ *18th May*

Are you qualified to confess someone else's sins? Then, don't gossip! Some of My children enjoy the glory of being the first with the news and being in the know; but see, My child, it will last only a moment and then a good friend may be lost, possibly forever! Is it worth it?

Instead, build each other up through the bad times. Hold your counsel unless it is asked for, and learn to be a good listener. A good friend will pass very little comment and never be judgemental. Many of My children are fragile and vulnerable, so be wary of making them feel worse. I will guide you if you just give them and their worries to Me.

James 1:26

"If you claim to be religious but don't control your tongue, you are just fooling yourself and your religion is worthless."

✝ *19th May*

If you continue in your unholy behaviour, how can you claim to be a Christian? Guard your temper and your tongue because this is the first line of action that others will see. It will colour their opinion of Me. Confirm your commitment to Me by changing your ways.

You must bring your behaviour into line with the new creation you have become. If you express My love and then your actions are detrimental towards one another, who then will want to be a Christian, or believe that you are a redeemed child of Mine?

Matthew 7:13-14

"You can enter God's kingdom only through the narrow gate. The highway to hell is broad, and it's gate is wide for the many who choose the easy way. But the gateway to life is small, and the road is narrow, and only a few ever find it."

✝ *20th May*

Many of my children worry. What can you change by worrying? Take a long, hard look at the priorities of your heart. What do you need to change? The main, important issue in your life should be the state of your soul. One day, My Son will come back for you and the world as you know it, will cease to exist! What use then are your worries? What will you have gained by them?

Establish Me firmly at the centre of your life and focus only on your eternal redemption. Serve Me with all of your heart and mind. Leave alone all that it is not in your power to change and concentrate on the things of Me.

Matthew 6:25 & 27

> *"Don't worry about every day life - whether you have enough food, drink, clothes. Doesn't life consist of more than food and clothing."*

> *"Can all your worries add a single moment to your life? Of course not."*

✝ *21st May*

Sexual temptation is a very potent thing and My children are not exempt from it. This society condones it when young people gain sexual experience before committing to marriage. Having many different partners is dangerous and can ruin a young life. Think very carefully, before going down a road that is paved with heartache.

Give your children cautious advice and try to be open with them on what is often deemed an embarrassing subject. It is worthwhile to share such topics with your child from a young age. It will enable you to have healthy discussions as your children grow. I understand the desires of the flesh.

Prayer

Dear Lord, give me the sensitive words necessary, in order to speak to my children about sexual morality. Help me to make this subject normal to discuss, without causing any embarrassment. Help me to point out the dangers and to teach them to wait until their bodies and emotions are ready. Show me how to prepare their fragile hearts and direct me to what your Word says on the subject. Amen.

✝ *22nd May*

I meet you at the point of your need. You are not always aware of the essence of your need. Worldly things occupy so much of your thoughts, but I search your heart and know the areas where you most need My input. I want to provide all that your heart desires, but those desires are not necessarily to your ultimate benefit.

Set your mind above such things and look at your real needs first. When those areas are catered for and your response is a spiritual desire to please Me, all these other wants will fade into insignificance. Raise your eyes above material and fleshly gratification.

Titus 2:12

> *"And we are instructed to turn from godless living and sinful pleasures. We should live in this evil world with self control, right conduct and devotion to God."*

✝ 23rd May

Don't be in awe of the gifts you don't have. Ask Me what you would like from My fruits. They are all available to you. In My wisdom I have already blessed you with an abundance of seeds; you need to concentrate on growing them.

Because you are unique and I know you so well, I have encouraged growth in the areas that fit your character perfectly. You have the fruits of My Spirit already, but the spiritual gifts you may ask for. I call each of you to serve Me in a different way. Concentrate on the talents I reveal in you and reap the rewards of knowing My hand is upon you.

Exodus 4:10-11

> *"Moses pleaded with the Lord, 'O Lord I am not a good speaker, I never have been and I'm not now, even after you have spoken to me I am clumsy with words.' 'Who makes mouths?' the Lord asked him, 'who makes people so they can speak or not speak, hear or not hear, see or not see. Is it not I the Lord? Now go and do what I have told you. I will help you speak well and I will tell you what to say.'"*

✝ 24th May

Some of My children have remained single, but all of you, married or not, have a family. All Christians are related through Christ. You are brothers and sisters together and are part of my Divine family. I love you all equally no matter where you fit into My church. Each one of you has a predestined purpose for your life and I will bless you in that realisation.

Whatever your mission in this life, it was ordained by Me. When you discover what I planned for you, the blessing surrounding that will flood from heaven. I spoke these words to My Son at His baptism, " 'This is My Son, in whom I am well pleased ...'" Let Me speak those words about you!

Prayer

Lord, show me how to know and accomplish your purpose for my life. Empower me to be willing to take a step of faith when your spirit reveals it to me. I welcome your blessings and am grateful that no matter which way you lead, I have your hand in mine and I will be successful with you. Amen.

✝ *25th May*

Be persistent in doing what you know is right. I will not close doors for you, unless going through them would cause you to be in grave danger. I have given you free will, so I won't interfere with your decisions. My child, you know right from wrong; My Spirit lives in you and He will lead but will never prevent something you are determined to do or have.

Your prayerful invitation will open doors for Me to warn you. This could be in something you read, hear from another, or sometimes it's the feeling My Spirit gives you, deep within your heart. Listen to My leading but ultimately the choice is yours.

Hebrews 5:14

> *"Solid food is for those who are mature, who have trained themselves to recognise the difference between right and wrong and then, do what is right."*

✝ *26th May*

My Son constantly intercedes on your behalf. He gave up His life in glory to save you. He came into the world in human form taking on all the restrictions that you have. He was born into poor circumstances, with the certain knowledge that He would be rejected and suffer a cruel death. His innocent blood was shed, out of love for a sinful world.

He made the ultimate sacrifice in giving His life for you. He understands all your emotions, distractions, temptations, physical disabilities, heartbreak, in fact everything that you go through, My Son has known first hand. Believe in Him and let Him help you.

Hebrews 2:17-18

"Therefore it was necessary for Jesus to be in every respect like us, his brothers and sisters, so he could be our merciful and faithful High Priest before God. He then could offer a sacrifice that would take away the sins of the people. Since he himself has gone through suffering and temptation, he is able to help us when we are being tempted."

✝ *27th May*

Some of you hear My voice, but you still rebel. This world did not happen by accident, yet some of you prefer to believe that it did.

My people wandered in the desert for 40 years covering very little ground. Don't make the same mistake. Hear My voice today, make a commitment to learn all you can about Me, place your trust in Me and follow with thanksgiving in your heart, believing what is true.

Hebrews 4:3

> *"For only we who believe can enter His place of rest. As for those who didn't believe, God said, 'In my anger I made a vow, they will never enter My place of rest.'"*

✝ 28th May

My child, examine your circumstances and don't give into false guilt - it will overwhelm you. Allow My Spirit to speak to you in truth. Search My Word for the answer; the knowledge you find there, will tell you what course of action will best please Me. My Spirit will convict you when your actions fall short of My standards.

Your feelings are not necessarily an accurate benchmark. Past experiences can load you down with feelings of guilt which could be completely unjustified. Tell Me what concerns you and do not punish yourself. If you are walking closely with Me, you must trust Me to be in all your circumstances.

Prayer

> *Lord, correct my wrong emotions as I give You a greater place in my life. I want to do what is right in Your sight. When I feel unsure about a course of action, lead me to the answer in Your Word. Protect my indiscretions from hurting someone else and give me a wise and discerning heart. In Jesus' name, Amen.*

✝ *29th May*

My child, you can have joy despite your problems. It's a joy that comes from within. Look to Me in all your circumstances, and with a thankful heart hold onto the joy that My peace brings. I am the source of all the good things in your life. My peace will release you from the bonds of slavery that has separated you from Me - those bonds of temper and discouragement, depressive moods and despondency.

Hand over all that binds you in spirit and look for the good in people and yourself. Try today to do one kind thing for another and gather up My blessings, ready to share again tomorrow.

Jeremiah 17:7

> *"But blessed are those who trust in the Lord and have made the Lord their hope and confidence."*

✝ 30th May

When you are obedient to Me, it is an expression of your love, not a fear of punishment. My child, we can have such a warm relationship. I long for you to be aware of My presence, and your desire to obey Me shows that you are. No friendship can work if it's only a one-way communication. I am here even when you are distracted in your busy life.

Begin each new day with Me, even before you open your eyes. Come with your plans and deposit your worries at the foot of the cross. My involvement in your everyday life means our closeness will grow beyond anything you could imagine. My laws for living must become second nature to you. When you fail, don't be despondent; confess and we will begin again together.

John 14:15-17

"If you love Me obey my commandments. And I will ask the Father and He will give you another counsel, who will never leave you. He is the Holy Spirit, who leads into all truth. The world at large cannot receive Him, because it isn't looking for Him, because it isn't looking for Him and doesn't recognise him. But you do because he is lives in you now and later will be in you."

✝ *31st May*

Take time, My child, to assess where you are going. Open your life to Me and I will guide you. There is never a moment when I am not aware of you and concerned for what is happening in your life. I want you to learn to leave your troubles with Me. Stop striving to manipulate things, that you really have no control over.

I want you to trust that I will never leave you. You are precious to Me and I will protect your path from becoming disastrous. Whatever happens at each turn, My heartfelt desire, is for you to include Me. I love to see you happy, but you must guard against neglecting your contact with Me. I want to be first in your life.

Prayer

Father, forgive me when I leave You out of my decision making, thinking that I know best. My mistakes teach me how much I need to rely on You, and that I need to include You, even in the little things in my life. I acknowledge that I am nothing without You. Thank You that You wait so patiently for me to remember that, Amen.

June

✝ 1st June

I know each beat of your heart, each breath that you take and all of your sorrows. My child, when you are feeling low, and everything feels out of balance, if your physical health isn't to blame, then examine your spiritual health. Tell Me what is troubling you. Everything that was dormant during the winter months, has now sprung into new life and the world looks a sunnier place.

If My creation doesn't uplift your spirit, then trust that My Word can. I am doing a new thing, I am putting you in position to be ready for what's around the corner, and Satan will fight Me on this. Be vigilant and lean on Me completely. As I make changes in you, I will supply all that you need, so trust Me and be ready.

Isaiah 43:19

"For I am about to do a new thing. See I have already begun! Do you not see it? I will make a pathway through the wilderness for my people to come home."

✝ 2nd June

I created you in minute detail. How could what I have created have happened by accident? How could the uniqueness of every living thing, have evolved from microscopic particles? Surely that would take more faith than believing in Me as the Creator? I took a rib from Adam's body and made Eve - nothing is impossible for Me.

The donkey that Jesus rode on, has a cross on his back, which is clear and distinctive. I have put a rainbow in the sky which appears after heavy downpours - a sign that I promise never to destroy the world again by flood. I resurrected My Son, and He sits at My right hand. I sent the Holy Spirit to be your counsellor and guide. I have blessed you with gifts and provided all that is good in the world. I love you!

Hebrews 11:3

"By faith we understand that the whole universe was formed at God's command, that what we now see did not come from anything that can be seen."

✝ *3rd June*

The most powerful testimony you can have is to live as an example to others. Be especially careful around unbelievers. As a member of My family, you may remain unaware of it, but you will be closely watched. If you explode with profanities, or pocket that pen you have taken from work, or fail to own up when you are undercharged, who is watching?

What about the testimony of omission? What if you don't help someone in need? If you don't behave in the way that Jesus taught you to, then what message does it send to the world? With patience and kindness, you will show that you are My child, so humble yourself before your fellow men. Live your life as if Christ were returning today.

1 Peter 2:12

> *"Be careful how you live among unbelieving neighbours.
> Even if they accuse you of doing wrong, they will see your
> honourable behaviour and they will believe and give
> honour to God when he comes to judge the world."*

✝ 4th June

Are you willing to study My Word so that you will know the truth? If you become familiar with the Bible, then you will have the ammunition necessary, to stand up for your faith. Don't allow false teaching to compromise what you have learned to be true.

Be wary of false teaching. It may seem logical but you must test everything against My Word. If a few false teachings are allowed to remain unchallenged, it will open the door for more. It will dull your sensitivity to the wrong path. I will give you the courage to speak out, but you must arm yourself with My Word.

2 John 1:7-8

"Many deceivers have gone out into this world. They do not believe that Jesus came to earth in a real body, such a person is a deceiver and an antichrist. Watch out so you do not lose the prize for which we have been working so hard. Be diligent so that you will receive your full reward."

✝ 5th June

My child, do you find it is difficult to admit when you are wrong? You waste so much time in self-justification when I would quickly forgive you and we could move on together. I never leave you alone. I sometimes have the need to distance Myself from your situation, but I never leave you. It enables you to evaluate the circumstances and maybe the cause.

Hindsight is a wonderful thing but if you keep your steps in line with Mine, it won't be necessary. Just as I don't interfere with your will, so My child, this law applies to you concerning others. Advice taken or given must be requested. Always be there for your friends, but quietly as I am, in the background. My child, learn from Me, and only get involved if invited.

Proverbs 25:11

"Timely advice is as lovely as golden apples in a silver basket."

✝ 6th June

Cooperation will ensure you live in harmony but you can still challenge the plans of others in a constructive way. Lose your aggression and aim to see all points of view. Team work joins you together in support of one another.

Each person involved can learn about reliance on others and yet still work on their own individual strengths. This will complement each of you. My church must learn unity in this way, as you work together with consideration. All My children will grow in My image. As you learn humility, you will gain strength in understanding the attitudes of one another.

1 Corinthians 1:10

Now, my dear brothers and sisters," I appeal to you by the authority of the Lord Jesus Christ, to stop arguing among yourselves. Let there be real harmony, so there won't be divisions in the church. I plead with you to be of one mind, united in thought and purpose."

✝ 7th June

You are special to Me! Believe My words, and don't allow anyone's criticism to destroy your self-worth. No one is justified in criticising someone else. I am the only judge who is qualified to make any assumption about you. I know you inside and out; your heart is crystal clear to Me. Concentrate on your commitment to Me and obey My commandments.

It is a favourite pastime for some who enjoy looking for the failure in others. All My children are gifted in different ways and you are not a failure because you don't shine at something. All I require from you is a willing heart and love for your neighbour. Repeat these words – 'God loves Me in whatever I do for Him'. I accept your heart and I will bless it.

Romans 14:4

"Who are you to condemn God's servants? They are responsible to the Lord, so let him tell them whether they are right or wrong. The Lord's power will help them do as they should."

✝ 8th June

My child, be humble in your behaviour towards others; you mustn't think that anyone is beneath you. If your attitude were that of a servant, your mind would be transformed by your service. You should have the attitude of Jesus when He washed His disciples' feet. He could have thought the task was demeaning, but no, He set an example, of the way in which I want you to treat one another.

Always put others' needs above your own, no matter who they are. Don't behave as the world does, only considering someone else after your own desires are satisfied. Be generous in your kindness and consider serving as a privilege.

John 13:14-15

"And since I the Lord and Teacher have washed your feet, you ought to wash each other's feet. I have given you an example to follow. Do as I have done to you."

✝ 9th June

I will bless your sacrifices to increase and supply the needs of others. Whatever you give is counted and multiplied even to the smallest amount and will be used in My Kingdom. The feeding of the 5,000 began with the selfless act of a small boy. He gave what he had to feed a multitude. He saw no obstacle when he offered everything.

How many of My children would be prepared to do the same? I use ordinary people to achieve great things. In My hands, you are amazing, but are you prepared to give whatever I ask, whatever the cost?

Malachi 3:10

"Bring all your tithes into the storehouse so there will be enough food in my temple. If you do," says the Lord Almighty, "I will open the windows of heaven for you. I will pour out a blessing so great you won't have enough room to take it in! Try it! Let me prove it to you."

✝ *10th June*

Remember, My child, you can't 'out-give' Me. I truly will bless abundantly all that you offer, when it is given with a pure heart. This includes your time and all your little kindnesses that you think go unnoticed but are seen by Me.

You are living the way that I want you to, when you are generous at every opportunity. You are then showing My love and blessing the lives of others. When you spend time in My presence, your desires will become a thing of beauty, as 'self' recedes into the background of your mind. I will sustain you as you become more like Jesus.

Luke 6:38

"If you give you will receive, your gift will be returned to you, in full measure, pressed down, shaken together to make room for more and running over."

✝ *11th June*

You don't need to be lonely since human company can never replace what we have together. I know that you also need the support of family and friends. Sometimes there are things you feel unable to share with even your closest contact. Bring these things to Me - I have an ever-listening ear.

Don't forget that I understand all that you are going through. I have the advantage that I can see the wider picture. I always have your best interests at heart and an hour with Me will lift your spirits and help you to put things in perspective. Don't let external pressures weigh you down; rather, bring your burdens to Me.

Deuteronomy 33:27

"The external God is your refuge and his everlasting arms are under you. He thrusts out the enemy before you; it is he who cries, 'destroy them.' "

✝ 12th June

Do you feel defeated? Don't make the mistake of thinking victory will come from material possessions. Your trust and obedience are the avenues to breakthrough. I understand how difficult your life can be. The decisions you have to make on a daily basis, can become a millstone around your neck.

I can release you from the bondage of fear and I will develop courage in you. Slowly, My child, you are changing as you allow Me into the grey areas. If you have invited Me into your worries and yet still make a bad judgement, don't despair. I will work it out for you, so trust Me. Your striving to accomplish what is right, will change the course of events if they are wrong.

Joshua 1:9

"I command you to be strong and courageous! Do not be afraid or discouraged. For the Lord your God is with you wherever you go."

✝ 13th June

My ways are not your ways. You often give up on Me because I do not act quickly enough, or according to your expectations. You misread My intentions and presume the course of action was a wrong one. You have free will! I am prepared to guide you in that will, but I will never make up your mind for you. Perseverance is something you must develop.

My child, I see that you want so much to please Me - that you stop and start so many ventures. Trust and be patient and when I am silent, don't mistake that for correction. You will be in no doubt when I do correct you, albeit gently. Our friendship is based on your faith! If you have involved Me, then do what you can and wait for Me to act.

Joshua 22:5

"But be careful to obey all the commands and the law that Moses gave to you. Love the Lord your God, walk in all his ways, obey his commands, be faithful to him and serve him with all your heart and all your soul."

✝ *14th June*

When your heart is feeling down and your spirit is low, review My past blessings. Recall all the times when you thought you were alone and remember My hand is always upon you. It will encourage you to carry on serving Me faithfully. Read all of My promises in the Bible and draw strength from My Word. Meditate on what I say.

Take time to appreciate My world. Take in the heady scent when you examine a beautiful flower; marvel over a spider's web - the sticky strength in the intricate weaving, designed to entrap her food. You needn't go far to enjoy the wonders of My creation. With a thankful heart, appreciate the comfort around you, the variety of food to satisfy and keep you healthy. But most of all, enjoy the freedom you have in Me.

1 Chronicles 16:8-9

> *"Give thanks to the Lord and proclaim his greatness. Let the whole world know what he has done. Sing to him, yes sing his praises. Tell everyone about his miracles."*

✝ 15th June

Are you prepared to allow Me full access in your life and trust that I will lead you? Do you believe that I am able to lead you in the best way possible? Your first steps as a young Christian, were well grounded in Me. As you grew and you became more confident in your faith, I gave you more freedom. It is only experience and a growing knowledge of Me which can build you up.

Our relationship is very much about trust, your trust in My judgement, over things that you are unable to control. When I see that your faith is increasing and you are ready to step out in that faith, I will honour it. Our ways of seeing things are different. But I know you inside out and I will protect you when you fall. You are My precious child.

1 John 2:24-25

"So you must remain faithful to what you have been taught from the beginning. If you do, you will continue to live in fellowship with the son and with the father. And in this fellowship we will enjoy the eternal life he promised us."

✝ *16th June*

My child, you will have different temptations than those of your neighbours - things that are testing and difficult to resist. Past experiences will help you, first of all to recognise them as temptations, and also to know how to avoid them. You cannot overcome these weaknesses on your own, the sooner you admit that this is in your flesh, the quicker you will be armed and ready to fight.

Make no mistake it will be a fight! The darkness in the world will try to convince you, that some sin is only a tiny thing; but small things grow into bigger things. You have boundaries for your children, because you want to protect them. I have boundaries for you too. My commandments are where those boundaries begin. My Word teaches you how to live your life.

1 John 5:18

"We know that those who have become part of God's family do not make a practice of sinning, for God's son holds them securely and the evil one cannot get his hands on them."

✝ 17th June

Adversity comes to all My children at various points in their lives. It comes under many guises and can be temporary or more disabling. How mature you are in your walk with Me, can and will help your response to these troubles. They will also help you to grow in maturity. At the time, My child, it can be very difficult but it will be very rewarding when you look back.

Climb over the hurdles with Me. I have equipped you with knowledge, resources, a biblical attitude and reasoning. The answer and the strength to overcome are found in Me. Give thanks to Me no matter what you are going through.

James 1:3-4

"For when your faith is tested, your endurance has a chance to grow. So let it grow, for when your endurance is fully developed, you will be strong in character and ready for anything."

✝ *18th June*

It is very hard for you not to retaliate. Verbal confrontation is quickly done and it can take a lifetime to undo, if that were indeed possible. The tongue is such a small part of the body, but runs away with words at such a rate, no one seems able to catch it. Look what damage occurs, when a thoughtless word is spoken, a fast retort that cuts deeply into another's soul.

The tongue can also bring healing and lift a spirit from the depths of despair. Wouldn't you rather that, My child, than plummeting someone into a painful self-doubt? It is so much better to refrain from speaking, than to let your tongue run away in harsh words - words that were probably unjustified in the first place.

James 3:8-9

"But no one can tame the tongue. It is an uncontrollable evil, full of deadly poison."

✝ 19th June

Let your faith shine out by showing your goodness to this unconcerned, cruel and indifferent world. Be ever watchful and uneasy, about the wrong done to others. Look out for injustice and achieve what you are able to on the behalf of those in need. In particular, be aware of those in abusive relationships, especially where children are involved.

Encourage the light to come into dark circumstances. For example, never doubt that a child is telling the truth since children aren't likely to make up stories of abuse. They will keep the secret about what is happening to them, because they think they won't be believed and often they are made to feel that it is their own fault. Look for signs among and help the helpless, and care for My little ones.

Ecclesiastes 4:1-3

> *"Again I observed all the oppression that takes place in the world. I saw the tears of the oppressed, with no one to comfort them. The oppressors have great power, and the victims are helpless."*

✝ 20th June

Do you know that I have holy hatred for sins committed against humanity. Focus your hatred on the sin, not on the perpetrators. Let Me judge them. I know that it feels alien to love those who have committed gross acts of wickedness, but that is what I ask you to do. Being My child means that you don't look down on others.

The things that are aberrant and disgust you, must be left with Me. Take care of the hurt and abused, do what you are able to, by standing out against evil; but recognise, My child, that there are some things which you can do nothing about. Leave those things with Me.

Luke 6:27-28

"But if you are willing to listen, I say, love your enemies. Do good to those who hate you. Pray for those who hurt you."

✝ *21st June*

I know that your faith will falter from time to time. You will suffer circumstances that will make you question. The answers you search for, are in My Word. When you face difficult, trying times in your life, it is then that I will cause you to grow. Your trusting faith in My care is a desire of My heart. I want you to know My heart.

Wait for My purpose to unfold during these hard times, but know that I will never leave you. I constantly watch over you, and you will find Me when you pray. Don't feel that you are in this alone, I will provide all that you need. Ask Me for help and draw on the strength and discernment that I will give to you.

1 Peter 5:10-11

> *"In his kindness God called you to his eternal glory by means of Jesus Christ. After you have suffered a little while, he will restore, support and strengthen you, and he will place you on a firm foundation. All power is his forever and ever. Amen."*

✝ *22nd June*

Let Me share your desolate thoughts. Changes to your circumstances and those of your loved ones will steal your joy if you let them. It is easy for someone looking in to offer unemotional advice, but you need to share your grief with a person who has been through a similar experience. Don't hold back from sharing your feelings. I will provide someone with empathy.

My heart is for the lonely and hurting. My child, you must lean on Me in your distress. Some of the things you are going through will drain you and deprive your mind of its rest. Snuggle in My arms and let all your fears and sadness be transferred to Me. I will carry your burdens.

Isaiah 43:2

"When you go through deep waters and great trouble, I will be with you."

✝ *23rd June*

My child, I will give you courage. You will never face adversity alone; My comforting hand will carry you above and beyond what you could ever have imagined possible. Look ahead with victory in your step. When your fears cause your legs to tremble, reach for My arm. Tell Me what is your 'Goliath'?

I will strengthen your resolve to overcome. Nothing that you face will overtake you, for we will meet it together. I will assist you when your fear threatens to be more powerful than your courage. I will increase your determination to succeed. Have faith that together, you and I can achieve anything you set your mind to, according to My will for you.

1 Samuel 17:45-46

> *"David shouted in reply, 'You come to me with sword, spear and javelin, but I come to you in the name of the Lord God Almighty - the God of the armies of Israel, whom you have defied. Today the Lord will conquer you.'"*

✝ 24th June

Your anxiety does you no credit. What use is it? Can it change anything that will happen? Tell Me - I am interested in all of your concerns. What troubles you is only a prayer away from My peace. Come constantly with your worries, I want to know about everything. Only by your giving Me access to these problems, can I intervene.

Watch for My direction, listen for My discernment which begins within your heart. I will speak to you in many ways. Trust that when you have a knowing deep inside, that it is My voice, prodding you into the right action. When once you have given your anxiety to Me, don't then take it back.

1 Thessalonians 5:16-18

"Always be joyful. Keep on praying. No matter what happens, always be thankful, for this is God's will for you who belong to Christ Jesus."

✝ *25th June*

Take some time just to be in My presence. Enjoy the early morning sun. Your mind is looking forward to a much-needed break. Your body needs to rest. Go and appreciate My world, take in all the summer smells and colours, that this season brings. The Spring lambs are growing up now, but they still have the exuberance of youth. I want to see your heart gamble in the way the lambs do.

Only by taking time away from your routine, or busy schedule, can you gather your resources and be ready to meet new challenges. So come with Me a while and rest, take stock. I will renew your spirit and your mind. Hold a wild flower in your hand and study it, marvel at its design. Each season brings new life - it grows, rests, increases, then begins again. How much more complex are you! Within My creation lies this simple lesson - that you need to recharge your batteries.

Isaiah 40:29

> *"He gives strength to those who are tired and worn out; he offers strength to the weak. Even youths will become exhausted, and young men will give up."*

✝ *26th June*

Don't let your emotions get the better of you. Saul lost the throne because of his jealous rages. It destroyed him on the inside and when he turned away from Me. He lost self-control and it manifested in his murderous intent towards David, someone he had loved. Address each negative emotion as soon as it appears, before it leads you into harm and actions you will regret.

Examine each new feeling as it occurs and decipher the reason for it. You will learn much about yourself and I will teach you to have self-control. Hasty reactions can destroy many relationships.

Prayer

> *Lord, help me to have control over my quick impulses.*
> *Encourage patience and a right attitude within me. I*
> *want to be a kind, peaceful person, who will always have*
> *considered responses. Forgive me when my actions hurt*
> *someone else, and give me the grace to say that I am sorry.*
> *Amen.*

✝ 27th June

Just as you are faithful to Me, be also faithful to your friends. Loyalty is a wonderful attribute and you must always, respect a confidence. The tongue likes to have its own way and likes to share what it knows. Learn to curb your desire to be the first one with the news. Secrets are not yours to tell!

It is far better to say nothing than to give your tongue free range. You will find the pleasure of gossip is short-lived and it will not do you justice. Be very careful, My child, to keep your counsel. If you gossip, let it be about Me.

Proverbs 26:20-22

"Fire goes out for lack of fuel and quarrels disappear when gossip stops. A quarrelsome person starts fights as easily as hot embers light charcoal or fire lights wood. What dainty morsels rumours are - but they sink deep into one's heart."

✝ *28th June*

Think about the things that you value, think how you take care of them, how important they are to you. That is the way I feel about you. Nothing can destroy or take away My protection for you. You are My very dear child and nothing you do can separate us. I love to see you happy, I do all that's unseen to encourage that.

Join with Me in fellowship and thanksgiving. I treasure our time together, I welcome you with open arms. Sometimes you are rushed, but don't let that stop you coming to Me. I am always here waiting for you. We can accomplish so much, if you have a willing heart. If you value anything, value your time with Me.

Revelation 3:20

"Look here I stand at the door and knock. If you hear me calling and open the door, I will come in, and we will share a meal as friends."

✝ 29th June

Have you lost your sensitivity to the joy and holiness of Me? Have you allowed other concerns to dull your spiritual senses? Does worshiping Me feel mundane and rob you of your energy? What has happened, My child? I want to reignite the flame within you. Confess your feelings and let Me help you.

Commit time to Me, delve deeper into My Word and put yourself in a position to be re-energised by My Spirit. Share your thoughts with other Christians, your church leader, and of course Me. All of My children go through barren times during their spiritual walk; I will wait patiently to renew and uplift your heart so you can recognise the things of Me.

Isaiah 55:1-2

> *"'Is anyone thirsty? Come and drink - even if you have no money! Come take your choice of wine or milk - it is all free! Why spend your money on food that does not give you strength? Why pay for food that does you no good? Listen, and I will tell you where to get food that is good for your soul!'"*

✝ 30th June

Don't put your trust in anything before Me! Money is necessary for your survival, but guard against your love of it. Your security is in Me, I am the source of all contentment. Nothing you can buy will give you everlasting satisfaction. Be grateful for My provision but learn to be thankful, no matter what.

You have wants and needs, but guard against your carnal nature, that relies on material things exclusively for your happiness. Joy comes from your obedient trust in Me. Be careful you don't become oblivious to the needs of others. Offer all that I give you, in order for Me to bless you in the service of others. I see your heart, My child, so let it please Me.

Matthew 6:24

"No one can serve two masters. For you will hate one and love the other, or be devoted to one and despise the other. You cannot serve both God and money."

July

✝ *1st July*

My child, come to Me in your sorrow; feel free to expose your heart in all its sadness. Your anguish runs deep and nothing anyone says can relieve your distress. Your painful emotions are My concern, so do not hesitate to lay down your suffering at the foot of the cross. Nothing you are experiencing is too personal for you to tell Me. I understand all your range of emotions.

It will help you just to be in My presence. When you feel ready, you can share those innermost thoughts with Me. None of your heartache should be your burden to suffer alone. I will comfort you, just rest a while, I understand. Bow your head and feel My hand in yours - there is healing in our silence together. My love for you is infinite.

Isaiah 66:13

"I will comfort you there as a child is comforted by its mother."

✝ *2nd July*

Loss is painful in whatever form it takes - whether bereavement, a broken romance, the decline of your health or old age and loss of ability. All are painful in their own right and no misery can be regarded as worse for one more than another. You all feel heartache at a personal level, sometimes in regret. My love will support you in many different ways.

Because you are My child, I know you individually, and I am best qualified to meet your need, and address your circumstances directly. Don't be afraid of your runaway emotions, they are difficult for you to cope with, but I have intimate knowledge of you and My compassion surrounds your life. Welcome those whom I send to you with support; they have first hand experience of similar suffering and will show empathy toward you.

Psalm 34:17-18

"The Lord hears his people when they call to him for help. He rescues them from all their troubles. The Lord is close to the broken-hearted, he rescues those who are crushed in spirit."

✝ *3rd July*

My child, are you ready to be a compassionate friend? The most helpful thing that you can do to remove your sadness, is to help someone else. This is probably the last thing on your mind and your fragility will make the prospect seem unattractive. Try and look past your heartache and see how the world is hurting.

Little steps will make a huge difference. My strength will sustain you. I will lift the veil of misery from your eyes and replace it with a sensitivity to want to render assistance to someone else. I will lift your heart and restore your joy in serving others. Don't be concerned if this takes time. By offering your resources or providing support in a practical way, it will open the door for Me to enter. Thank you, My child.

Psalm 72:12-14

"He will rescue the poor when they cry out to Him; He will help the oppressed, who have no one to defend them. He feels pity for the weak and the needy, and He will rescue them. He will save them from oppression and violence, for their lives are precious to Him."

✝ 4th July

Can you see the difference your shared love has made, to how you feel about yourself? My Son died for you to learn to live in this unselfish way. You are obeying the greatest commandment. Love one another! If the world would begin to do this, all this heartache would be a thing of the past. It would be therapy for your soul.

Misfortune would be shared and thereby overcome with ease of mind and heart. Love breeds love, as it touches and spreads. Oh, if My children would only apply this to their lives, tears would be dried and joy would become contagious, instead of this dark cruelty which destroys. Reach out to one another, embrace all problems together and let compassion seep deeply into your souls.

Matthew 7:12

> *"Do for others what you would like them to do for you. This is a summary of all that is taught in the law and the prophets."*

✝ *5th July*

Are you desperate for someone to love you? Have you lost someone important? Lean on Me and I will help your suffering heart. Time will dull the memory, it can also enhance the good times. Dwell on those happy days that were filled with joy - they will come again. Trust that I have a purpose for your life and when you are ready, I will reveal it. Take great comfort from knowing that your name is written on My hand.

These days may be poignant ones, as you wait for My plans to be revealed. Nothing will happen to you that hasn't been allowed by heaven first. I will never let you fall. Tell Me how you feel and what the desire of your heart is. Pray in compliance with My will and power will be released from heaven. Be ever-watchful and act when I bring new situations before you. Be expectant.

Job 22:28

> *"Whatever you decide to do will be accomplished, and light will shine on the road ahead of you."*

✝ 6th July

Have your words hurt someone? Are you wallowing in self-pity because you felt justified in what you said to them? You need to ask forgiveness, not only from Me, but also from them. Let Me decide who needs My judgement which will ensue if they don't repent. Don't harbour your hurts until they fester and become cankerous. It will do harm to your soul and separate us.

With the damage caused from your experience with others, I will build you up. When you are fragile and you have the need to blame, it won't help your heart to accuse. Take My love and let Me nurse you through this hard, emotional time. You must speak your forgiveness, even though your heart doesn't feel it; in time, with My healing, it will become so.

Luke 17:4

"Even if he wrongs you seven times a day and each time turns again and asks forgiveness, forgive him."

✝ 7th July

I understand when you are tempted to do wrong. Jesus spent 40 days and 40 nights in the desert being tempted by Satan. I can see the areas where you are most vulnerable; indeed all of My children have weaknesses. Sin entered through Adam so opening the door to all temptations. Corruption is all around you and I see your constant battle.

My Son fights for you, but you must cooperate. I will strengthen you to resist evil; but unless you have a strong desire to do what is right and follow Me, the battle will weary you. Arm yourself against Satan, put on My spiritual armour, read My Word and pray into every situation.

1 Corinthians 10:13

"But remember that the temptations in your life are no different from what others experience. And God is faithful he will keep the temptation from becoming so strong that you can't stand up against it. When you are tempted, he will show you a way out so that you will not give in to it."

✝ 8th July

Forgiveness is fundamental to your faith. I know you find it difficult, but look inside yourself to discern any feelings of guilt. Wouldn't you want those feelings to be quickly dispelled? If you can offer that to another, why wouldn't you do it? The result will be a lightness in your step, a release in your spirit. Think how desperately you want that for yourself.

It is easier to condemn than to take on responsibility. How would your life be affected if others were to treat you in this way? Don't harden your heart as Pharaoh did - look what punishment he incurred! My heart is to forgive instantly, and unconditionally, in an overwhelming desire to show you love. Please, My child, do the same for others.

Numbers 14:19

"Please pardon the sins of this people because of your magnificent, unfailing love."

✝ *9th July*

Your heart is fragile, so why not let Me minister to you. I don't want you to withdraw inside yourself. By My power and might you can stand up to these difficult circumstances. You are never in this war alone; stretch out your spirit to meet Mine. There is an invisible thread that joins us. It is strong and reliable, nothing can break it. When you offered your life to Me, I immediately took action to secure you.

My protective shield surrounds you and you need never be afraid of losing Me. I see the struggles you have, sometimes the fog blinds you to My presence. Make your first words of the day be to Me, and I will lift your heart and make the sun shine upon you. I will heal your hurts, despair will be foreign to you. Stay close to Me, and I will never let you go.

2 Corinthians 4:7-8

"But this precious treasure - this light and power that now shines within us - is held in perishable containers, that is, in our weak bodies. So that everyone can see that our glorious power is from God and is not our own. We are pressed on every side by troubles, but we are not crushed and broken. We are perplexed but we don't give up and quit."

✝ 10th July

I am your God. I am tender and just, and My yearning is to have closer fellowship with you. I will not compromise. Our journey is unpredictable to you, but I take all that happens and weave it in and out of the goodness that I placed within you. Let your worries fade away as we face each new challenge together. The Comforter will guide you; listen to His leading - it comes from Me.

Come, let us re-direct that stubborn streak into something positive. Release all that weighs you down into My care and allow Me to work. Your clouded view and unforgiveness do you an injustice. I know your heart, My child, I see the dissolution that damages My plans. Try to accept the things you are unable to influence and leave them with Me.

Proverbs 3:5-6

"Trust in the Lord with all your heart; do not depend on your own understanding. Seek his will in all you do and he will direct your paths."

✝ 11th July

Do not ignore the distress your actions are able to cause. Put yourself in another's position and feel the pain before you give way to your fleshly desires. Yes, you may seem to get away undetected, but I see all things. I have given you a gentle, sensitive heart, so be mild-mannered and aware that what you do will affect others. The excitement of a new relationship is intense, but if it's not with one who is free, it will become toxic.

I understand the temptations of the heart, but be careful, My child, they can bruise you and damage friendships irreparably. Sexual desire is a positive instinct. I made you to be this way in a committed relationship. Take nothing that belongs to another. Guard against your rampant desires which are caused by your carnal nature; they will be hard to resist because, from the beginning of time, men and women have seduced one another.

1 Thessalonians 4:3-4

"God wants you to be holy, so you should keep clear of sexual sin. Then each of you will control your body and live in holiness and honour - not in lustful passion as the pagans do, in their ignorance of God's ways."

✝ 12th July

Come to Me and I will strengthen you in those areas that you are weakest. All My children have 'grey areas' where they convince themselves that they are not really doing wrong. All sins are wrong! You should not grade them. For example, a lie cannot be white. The corruption that took place in the garden has increased, and you must be ever-vigilant against the powers of darkness which seek to take you from Me.

My Spirit is consistently working within you. The pull you feel deep inside must be responded to. Listen to the conviction of My voice when you are tempted. Remove yourself from situations that will tempt you more. You know what it means to long for something that, in your heart of hearts, is against all that I stand for. Let Me help you to overcome, but you must really want to.

1 John 2:16

"For the world offers only the lust for physical pleasure, the lust for everything we see and pride in our possessions. These are not from the father. They are from this evil world."

✝ 13th July

Do you struggle with doubt? Life with Me is all about faith. Your spiritual well-being is very important to Me; I will teach you to trust Me. Your faith will become real as a result. I can change anything in your life, but to do so immediately, would not be good for you, even if it would increase your faith. Pray from your heart and in line with My will and it will be so.

Are you willing to follow My guidelines which are outlined in My word? Do you believe in your salvation? Are you willing to suffer for Me? If you can answer yes to these questions, then you are growing in a relationship with Me. Faith will follow.

Hebrews 11:6

"So you see it is impossible to please God without faith.
Anyone who wants to come to him must believe that there
is a God and that he rewards those who sincerely seek
him."

✝ *14th July*

I can remove that heavy burden of stress that weighs you down. Many are My ways of doing this. When you can stagger no longer, put down your load at the foot of the cross. Take the hope that I offer you, it is given freely. Now speak these words - "I belong to the Lord Jesus Christ. He is my Saviour, my Friend - I will follow Him without question."

When life becomes a drudge and you can see no earthly end to your struggles, look to heaven and your salvation. I am consistently working on your behalf, putting into place things that you keep stepping over. Don't let the trials of this life take away the joy of looking forward to the next. Hang on to what Jesus did for you.

John 3:16

"For God so loved the world that he gave his only son, so that everyone who believes in him will not perish but have eternal life."

✝ 15th July

My child, give up that which is separating us. You know what it is because My Spirit has been nudging and convicting you. To carry on doing in secret, what is wrong, will eventually destroy you. Decay spreads and damages all that it touches. A snail eats the things that are rotting on the woodland floor, but do you know what stench the snail gives off when his body is damaged?

Your wrongs will separate you from Me, and the stench of sin will seep from your soul. My healing touch of forgiveness, if coupled with your remorse, will remove the worse possible decay and begin new growth. Have courage, My child, to look ahead and not backwards. Little steps with Me will change the direction of your life.

Psalm 51:1-2

"Have mercy on me, O God, because of your unfailing love. Because of your great compassion, blot out the stain of my sins. Wash me clean from my guilt. Purify me from my sin."

✝ *16th July*

You have My protection, so don't be afraid when I don't always intervene. I will work it out for your good. It is sometimes necessary for you to encounter things in your life, in order for Me to teach you and then you will grow. You mustn't feel that I don't care when those problems you ask Me to remove, remain with you. Life is an experience and I want you to enjoy it.

Each trial will have a lasting impression because we will work through them together. It is often in preparation for another season of your life. I not only use these events to encourage you to grow spiritually, but also to benefit others who in time will need your empathy, when they have a similar experience. This will strengthen My church.

Galatians 6:2

> *"Share each other's troubles and problems, and in this way obey the law of Christ."*

✝ *17th July*

Healing is a really difficult subject for you to believe in. Don't accept it when someone says, "Well, it must be God's will," in response to your continuing suffering. My will is for you to enjoy life and live it to the full, that doesn't just mean spiritual matters. My intention is for your body to be as healthy as your soul. Does that cause you to feel uncomfortable? Is there something in your heart that doesn't align with My will? Does it scare you to think of your body being the same?

Let us first address these inner turmoils. Don't think that I won't heal the body if the heart isn't right; but My first desire is that you and I are one. Have faith, My child, and come to Me with expectation and gratitude. I want you to trust Me in all things. If I leave your body with disabilities, then I have a purpose. It is biblical to ask for healing.

James 5:14

> *"Are any among you sick? They should call for the elders of the church and have them pray over them, anointing them with oil in the name of the Lord. And their prayer offered in faith will heal the sick, and the Lord will make them well."*

✝ 18th July

Allow your vulnerability to show to your Christian brothers and sisters. Make no apology for your weakness. All My children are vulnerable, so why not let Me be your strength. I do not see you as the world sees you. I will minister to you in your struggles, but in order to receive true fellowship within My church, you must be honest with those you feel are trustworthy.

There are areas in which you are susceptible, but in a loving environment you must not fear criticism. All of My children have a deep need to be understood, without judgement. The body of My church has many skills and your weakness will be another's strength. This is why when you work together as one body, great and wonderful things can be achieved.

1 Corinthians 12:27

"Now all of you together are Christ's body, and each one of you is a separate and necessary part of it."

✝ *19th July*

Are you satisfied with your life? Is there anything that you would like to change? Come and tell Me of your regrets. Maybe there is something you would have done differently, but now you feel that it is too late, or the damage is done and you must live with it. Yes, My child, some things cannot be altered and you must accept the consequences, but that doesn't mean that you can't change what will happen next.

Lay out all that has occurred, and all that may result from your unskilled planning or mistakes. I can alter the course of anything. If you represent Me in a way that makes Me proud, I will intervene on your behalf. I am the all-powerful God who loves you and wants the best for you. Hand over all those worries and concerns to Me, and watch as I work on your behalf.

Prayer

> *Father, give me wisdom in making decisions that will affect my future. Make me tenacious for You. When I continue down the wrong road, please bring me back. Help me to view my life with a critical eye, due to the mistakes I have made. Show me how to put things right, as I walk closer and closer to you. Amen.*

✝ *20th July*

Talk to Me, My child, so that I can help you. I can see when you feel out-of-sorts which can create distance between us. Nothing you tell Me will shock Me. I am aware of all your concerns, but unless you allow Me in, how can I reach you? The mountain you are trying to climb will overpower you without My help.

What seems frightening and tragic is a mere hiccup to Me. Stop your fretting and look to Me for the solution. I may not respond to your problem in the way you would like, but when you look back, you will concede that it was for the best.

Psalm 66:17-19

"For I cried out to Him for help, praising Him as I spoke.
If I had not confessed the sin in my heart, my Lord would
not have listened! But God did listen, He paid attention
to my prayer."

✝ *21st July*

I am always here, My child, waiting in the background for you to share with Me. When you feel that your life is unravelling, come and rest with Me. Life is full of peaks and troughs - some of your own making, some caused by outside influences. Allow Me to be at the bottom and also the top. I long to share everything in your life.

Make a space for Me. I am not angry with your failures. I love you deeply and your hurts are of deep concern to Me. You will be able to feel peace in the direst of circumstances. My Spirit will calm you and you will still be able to thank Me, even in the middle of chaos. Trust that I will truly work everything out for your good.

Prayer

> *Father thank you that you touch my circumstances. You*
> *work tirelessly in my life and I am mainly unaware*
> *of it. When I look back I can see Your hand, wisdom,*
> *and compassion. Thank You, for never letting me down.*
> *Strengthen me so I will become the person you made me to*
> *be. Amen.*

✝ *22nd July*

Enjoy the warm, lazy, summer days. Drink in the beauty of the colourful gardens. Let the birdsong enchant you, relax to the hum of the insects, busily going about their work. The freshly-mown grass is a spectrum of vibrant green, tantalisingly fragrant as the scent reaches you. I purposefully created all this with careful planning - none of it was by accident.

I foresaw all that would happen in the world and yet I loved you enough to prepare a way for you. When you deviate from My path, it grieves My Spirit. I am always ready to bring you back. A contrite heart is all it takes. Examine what you do often and through our intimate relationship, you will know when your step has faltered.

Jeremiah 3:22

> *"'My wayward children,' says the Lord, 'come back to me, and I will heal your wayward hearts.'"*

✝ 23rd July

My Son paid a high price for your sin - you need not feel guilty. It is very hard for you to admit when you do something wrong. That includes admitting your iniquities to Me and sometimes to others. You will have to humble yourself - this doesn't come naturally, and you have to die to self. The rewards are great - restored relationships, peace and a release from your sin.

Pride is a very powerful emotion and will always colour your view concerning the facts. Is your guilt or your pride going to get the better of you? Don't isolate yourself from Me and significant others who are in a position to help. Look to the pure heart that I keep placing in you following your repentant confessions.

John 15:10

"In the same way, there is joy in the presence of God's angels when even one sinner repents."

✝ 24th July

Commitment is exclusive and costly. Be prepared and understand this, in your relationships. When you invited My Spirit to come and live within your heart, in effect you became betrothed to My Son. The human heart understands this level of commitment. The promise you made, in My presence, was to be faithful. This corrupt world tries, at every turn, to undermine that bond of fidelity, and it is very challenging for you.

Your promise shows Me your faithfulness. Just as in a good marriage, though your freedom is restricted, you no longer think only of yourself. I expect a distinct level of obedience from you. As you spend more time with Me, our friendship will become more intimate. You will develop a new dedication to pleasing Me.

Luke 14:26

> *"If you want to be my follower you must love me more*
> *than, your own father and mother, wife and children,*
> *brothers and sisters - yes more than your own life.*
> *Otherwise you cannot be my disciple."*

✝ *25th July*

If you are found lacking in the small things, it will open the door for dishonesty in larger things. An open door allows all kinds of unwanted things to enter. The darkness allows them to come in undetected, until the room is full of things which are unwanted. How then, My child, can you differentiate between good and evil? Take care never to leave the door ajar.

Your integrity must be worn like a sign - it should be what defines you. I am being removed from so many places, under the pretext of 'freedom of choice'. Make your choices around My commandments, and adhere to them strictly. If you are ever in doubt about where I stand on something, ask Me, and read what I say in My Word.

Luke 11:25-26

> *"When an evil spirit leaves a person, it goes into the desert, searching for rest. But when it finds none, it says, 'I will return to the person I came from.' So it returns and finds that its former home is all swept and clean. Then the spirit finds seven other spirits, more evil than itself, and they all enter the person and live there. And so that person is worse off than before."*

✝ 26th July

One day, My child, I will bring you home to be with Me. The suffering of this world will be no more. I have promised you everlasting life and freedom from the earthly body that has confined you. Some of you who suffer will be released from pain and infirmities, but all of you will have a new body without the restrictions that you now endure.

There will be no more death and decay! I am changing you to become like My Son. Your spirit will live on, I will resurrect you to live in heaven with Me. You have salvation in Jesus Christ. You are no longer captive to the power of darkness, but now you are saved. My Spirit lives in you!

Romans 8:22-23

"For we know that all creation has been groaning as in the pains of childbirth right up to the present time. And even we Christians, although we have the Holy Spirit within us as a foretaste of future glory, also groan to be released from pain and suffering. We too wait anxiously for that day when God will give us our full rights, as his children, including the new bodies he has promised us."

✝ 27th July

Where does your contentment come from? Are you still relying on yourself? Don't you see that you can be content, no matter what you may be struggling with. If you include Me, then My peace will reign in your life. Your experiences are a continual learning process. Choose how you intend to react in every circumstance.

I enjoy sharing all things with you, I enjoy seeing your reaction when I bless you. Anticipate My blessings - they are readily available and it gives Me great joy to give you good things. Your ability to cope with life will come from Me whatever your situation. Choose to be joyful.

Philippians 4:12

"I know how to live on almost nothing or with everything.
I have learned the secret of living in every situation,
whether it is will a full stomach or empty, with plenty or
with little."

✝ *28th July*

Be concerned, but not too alarmed, by the horrors that are taking place in the world today. These events signify that Satan has a very firm foothold. Don't allow him to steal your peace. Be ever alert to his deceit! It is only by going back to My Word, that you can live with hope. My promises are true, and you can whisper them to Me each day, not because I forget, but to keep you from forgetting. Remember that you are saved and salvation awaits you through My Son.

My Word has predicted the events that are taking place right now. Some of the forecasts remain sealed. I have shortened the days in order that you can survive them. Place everything in My hands, especially what you are unable to change. Trust that light will come into the darkness. We are in a battle, so put on My armour.

Daniel 12:4

"But you Daniel keep this prophesy secret; seal up the book until the time of the end. Many will rush here and there, and knowledge will increase."

✝ *29th July*

Do you believe that I have your future in My hands, and that I have a purpose for your life? If you are still waiting to discover what that purpose is, then spend time in deep prayer with Me. If you have begun many ventures and they have been less than successful, accept that they were never in My plan.

I will never stop you doing what you have set your mind on, even if it interrupts or delays My Plan. Instead I will sometimes weave it into My purpose. Your free will makes you an individual, but I want you to freely submit it to Me! I love to see the plans of your heart. If they fit well with My intentions, then they are excellent. I will always work towards a satisfactory result, even when you deviate.

Prayer

Lord, when I go off at a tangent doing my own thing, please bring me back. Speak into every situation in my life, guide me through the mud, when I can't see Your hand clearly. Teach me to listen and align my will with yours. Amen.

✝ 30th July

The more time you spend with Me, the clearer My voice will become. Tell Me what troubles you in your life. My child, don't struggle alone. Bring your worries and limitations straight to Me, for what can be gained by bottling them up? Even the tiniest detail of your life concerns Me and I long to be involved.

Focus on the good points that you have and develop them abundantly. For example, focus on the good things about your spouse and the negative things will recede. None of My children are perfect, but I love you all unconditionally. Try that unconditional love with each other.

Ephesians 3:18-19

"And may you have the power to understand as all
God's people should, how wide, how long, how high,
and how deep his love really is. May you experience the
love of Christ though it is so great you will never fully
understand it. Then you will be filled with the fullness of
life and power that comes from God."

✝ *31st July*

Take time to consider where you want to go with your life. The summer months are here to enjoy, but don't leave the fields fallow for too long. It is always good to gather your thoughts and consider a new direction. Enjoy contentment, as the hazy sunshine warms your limbs. Look back over your achievements during the last few months and consider where you have placed Me.

Have you left Me out of things? Have you been too busy satisfying yourself, or that new special person in your life? It's time to take stock and get more involved with Me. I am waiting to be included, once you are rested. Regroup and let's see what new things we can accomplish together.

Isaiah 43:20

"The wild animals in the fields will thank me, the jackals and ostriches too, for giving them water in the wilderness. Yes I will make springs in the desert, so that my chosen people can be protected."

August

✝ *1st August*

I have given you the necessary strength to develop self-control. Sometimes your determination is weak; there are many reasons that can cause this. I understand your heart and I see the inward struggles you have. You must come to a point where the goal you have set yourself is a prize worth winning. How much do you want to control your desires and emotional instability?

Come, talk to Me about these things, I can strengthen you beyond your wildest dreams. Self-control is attainable with Me, but, you must really want what you are aiming for. Dependence on worldly things will increase your tendency to sin. If you keep giving in, you will form a habit, and habits are very difficult to break. I can help you achieve victory.

2 Peter 1:6

"Knowing God leads to self control. Self control leads to patient endurance and patient endurance leads to Godliness."

✝ 2nd August

You will become more godly when you allow Me to work in you. Have you ever experienced a horse being broken in? The horse has got to submit to its master and allow the bit to be placed between its teeth. It doesn't come easily to the horse because it has spirit and the cold metal feels alien in its mouth. There comes a time though when it feels the comfort of the familiar feeling of being led.

I see your struggles, your wilfulness and your need to be independent. Allowing Me into your whole life won't take those things away, but like the horse you will have a new Master. You will start to welcome your dependency on Me - it will make you feel safe. You will never feel alone again, and you will be stronger.

Job 22:21-22

> *"Stop quarrelling with God! If you agree with him you*
> *will have peace at last and things will go well for you.*
> *Listen to his instructions and store them in your heart.*
> *If you return to the Almighty and clean up your life, you*
> *will be restored."*

✝ *3rd August*

Don't be like those who find their joy in materialism. Their joy is short-lived and they quickly move onto the next thing on their wish list. Are they ever going to be satisfied? Your joy is in Me! Unless you have an intimate relationship with Me, you will never understand that. I want so very much to bless you. I want to steer you to a path of peace.

The things you acquire will be of no use when you die; you truly can't take them with you. Give away the clutter in your life, not just material things, but also the clutter that keeps you from Me - the unhelpful pastimes that occupy you and open the door for dangerous thoughts. Be aware of what you read or watch on TV. I only warn you so that you won't give a foothold to Satan.

Matthew 6:19-21

> *"Don't store up treasures here on earth, where they can be eaten by moths and get rusty and where thieves break in and steal. Store your treasures in heaven, where they will never become moth eaten or rusty and where they will be safe from thieves. Wherever your treasure is, there your heart and thoughts will be also!"*

✝ *4th August*

It's hard for you to love your enemies, yet I want you to do this! Whether it is in the playground or between great nations, the result is a peaceful course of action. You don't want conflict, My child - it is unproductive and tears My people apart. You have seen the physical injuries caused by war, but how much more the mental and spiritual injuries which are unseen.

The heartache of verbal war in your homes, within families, is a root of aggression. Teach your children to talk, apologise, and find some common ground for a peaceful solution. Don't ever allow arguments to spiral out of control. Be a peacemaker, and stop at its source what will fester into decay.

Matthew 5:43-44

> *"You have heard that the law of Moses says, Love your neighbour and hate your enemy. But I say, Love your enemies! Pray for those who persecute you."*

✝ *5th August*

I have forgiven you! Having experienced my forgiveness, you must pass on your forgiveness to others! When you are deeply hurt, it is very hard to say those words. Even if your heart doesn't feel forgiveness yet, take some action to show Me that you are trying. I will bless what I see in the silent place within your heart, and your forgiveness will become a reality.

My child, your complex emotions prevent so many of My blessings from taking effect. You miss them because you are occupied elsewhere. You find it difficult to admit when you are at fault. Ask Me to show you when you are wrong and how you can best put it right. Learn from Me how to live in harmony with others.

Romans 12:16

"Live in harmony with each other. Don't try to act important, but enjoy the company of ordinary people. And don't think you know it all!"

✝ *6th August*

You are not responsible for the happiness of others. However, by your actions, you may be responsible for making them unhappy. Consider how you make people feel when they are around you. People who make others laugh - with their humour - are like a magnet. Not everyone has that gift.

Each of My children does have a special gift though and as part of the body of Christ, you should use it to bless others. You have a duty to live a morally just life, to treat each other with respect and servanthood. Use My love to bring others to Me.

Psalm 1:1-2

> *"Oh the joys of those who do not follow the advice of the wicked, or stand around with sinners, or join in with scoffers. But they delight in doing everything the Lord wants; day and night they think about his law."*

✝ *7th August*

My child, your earthly parents taught you many things. One of the important things in this life, is wisdom, so develop a thirst for it. I will teach you, as you become reverent towards Me and My Word. Think deeply about the Proverbs that Solomon and others wrote. They are not My laws, but a revelation for helping you in your daily life.

Wisdom (as opposed to many of your attributes which are genetic), needs to be learnt. Experience teaches you many things, not all them good, but by applying the Proverbs to your life, you will be saved from many downfalls. Read and study them.

Proverbs 12:1

> *To learn you must love discipline; it is stupid to hate correction."*

Cheating will bring war into your soul. I see all that you do in secret, whether it is good or bad. You grieve the Holy Spirit when you become steeped in deceit. Any form that this takes, however small your offence appears to you, is a corruption of My ways. If you do things that have to be hidden, then by the 'nature of darkness', you know they are wrong.

Turn back, My child, and come to Me. Admit your guilt, ask for forgiveness and ask for My strength, to be able to resist recommitting those things. I see those strong temptations that you face on a daily basis. I hear your friends justifying their giving into temptation. You are My child! Do not be swayed by the encouragement of others.

Romans 14:12-13

"Yes each of us will have to give a personnel account to God."

✝ *9th August*

Before you speak, be aware of every word you intend to say. Don't allow your tongue to have its own way. It is the hardest of muscles to control. Your words can cause conflict, stress, hurt and guilt; but look what joy and kindness they can bring. Wouldn't you rather they were uplifting others, rather than knocking them down?

Cast your mind back to your childhood. Can you remember, with accuracy, the words a teacher spoke to you? Many of My children have been damaged by the thoughtless criticism they received. Be sensitive in your outspokenness, and imagine that you were hearing some of the things that you say, being aimed towards you. If you humbly seek My guidance, I will help you to curb your tongue.

Proverbs 15:4

"Gentle words bring life and health; a deceitful tongue crushes the spirit."

✝ *10th August*

You need to rest, My child. I am pleased by all that you do for Me; but I never intended that you would work so hard, that you would wear yourself out. Learn that you have the ability to say 'No'. I see the nature you have developed to want to please everyone. But agreeing to do everything that you are asked to do, causes people to have unreal expectations of you.

You have set a precedent by being too willing. Your involvement is pleasing, but only if you are enjoying it. When the demands become too great, you will begin to resent it. It doesn't matter that people will feel let down; you are not letting Me down when you say 'No'. Rather, you are saving time for your relationship with Me and protecting your health.

Prayer

> *Father, help me to recognise the things You wish me to be*
> *involved in and to have the strength of character to refuse*
> *to take on those things that You haven't asked me to do.*
> *Please give me clear guidance to know the difference. In*
> *Jesus' name, Amen.*

✝ *11th August*

If your thoughts are left unchecked, they can easily slip out of control. Adultery is rife in this modern world and marriage vows are so easily taken for granted. Divorce comes to mind so quickly and some even seem to marry with that in mind. I made you to be physical beings, but lust is a ready evil and is planted by visual things. Guard against all that would lead you down that road.

You can admire beauty in others; that is quite different from fantasising about a sexual relationship with them. Look after your spouse and address any problems in your marriage that would cause you to have a roving eye. The first flush of excited love should grow into a happy contentment. Revive your marriage with love and do not deny each other a loving, sexual relationship.

Hebrews 13:4

"Give honour to marriage and remain faithful to one another in marriage. God will surely judge people who are immoral and those who commit adultery."

✝ *12th August*

You can and must discipline yourself into doing what is right. If you discipline yourself, it honours Me. When My Spirit is living in your heart, He will lead you and your love for Me means that you will want to obey My commandments. If you live this way, doing what is right will come naturally to you as breathing.

My child, don't be lulled for a minute into believing you will always do what is right in My sight. There will always be distractions and temptations. You must continually ask for My direction, in each new situation that you face. I am pleased that you include Me and you will find My path to be straight and narrow. If you lose self-discipline, then ask Me to strengthen you in that area.

Hebrews 12:7

"As you endure this Divine discipline, remember that God is treating you as his children. Who ever heard of a child who was never disciplined?"

✝ 13th August

I will use your suffering to deepen your faith. You will have to endure many testing times, in your life. These times will take many forms and you can chose how you deal with them. Use these difficulties to grow closer to Me. When the storms come, I want you to rely totally on Me. Reaching out to Me will prove how much I mean to you.

You know, My child, what you mean to Me! If you are in any doubt, the 'eye of the storm' will convince you. But Only by faith and trust in Me, will I be able to give you peace, in the most dire of circumstances. If you are tempted to go it alone, I will wait for you to turn around and reach out to Me. In the most battering flood, I will be there with a boat.

Psalm 18:19-20

"He led me to a place of safety; he rescued me because he delights in me. The Lord rewarded me for doing right; he compensated me because of my innocence."

✝ *14th August*

My child, you can always rely on My mercy. I will always forgive a contrite heart, but you must be sorry. Why waste time wallowing in self-pity and guilt? I know you do wrong, but make sure your heart doesn't relish those things that displease Me. Why hold onto your feelings of guilt when you can come to Me for forgiveness? My mercy won't extend to your heart, if it's just for a quick fix.

Your mistakes can be forgiven, but I am alerted to repeated offences. If you are coming to Me, just to be spared the consequences of your sin, then should I show you mercy? I want you to let My mercy change you! If I see that you are sorry, but will soon put yourself in the same position once again, you will have to accept My discipline. My teaching is gentle but firm.

Deuteronomy 13:18

"The Lord your God will be merciful only if you obey him and keep all the commands I am giving you today, doing what is pleasing to him."

✝ *15th August*

Your tithing pleases Me, but be aware that all you have is from My provision and you must use it wisely. True giving cannot be forced and is always driven by love. Thank you, My child, for all that you give back to Me. When your motivation is one of selfless giving, there is great joy in heaven.

I will give you a heart of compassion for My hurting people and more than enough for your needs. Look around you and search out those that I want you to help. The world has many in it who have nothing. Charities spring up all the time, and good people who care are fundraising. What are you prepared to do, My child?

2 Corinthians 9:11

"Yes you will be enriched so that you can give even more generously. And when we take your gifts to those who need them, they will break out in thanksgiving to God!"

✝ *16th August*

There are suffering souls on the streets - people who have nothing, who live cold, lonely lives. Are you willing to help them? Do you believe those who say their circumstances are their own fault? If this is the case, does that make any difference? Have I not given you a heart of compassion? Did I leave you where I found you? No, My child, I cared for you, fed, clothed and loved you!

These hurting people are My sheep, and they need to be brought back to the flock. Give them your time, and nestle them in My love. Whatever their story, you must not judge; whatever they do to survive in a hostile world, do you think they have a choice? Will you be My hands to help meet their needs?

Luke 10:30-32

"A Jewish man was travelling on a trip from Jerusalem to Jericho and he was attacked by bandits. They stripped him of his clothes and money, beat him up and left him half dead, beside the road. By chance a Jewish priest came along, but when he saw the man lying there, he crossed to the other side of the road and passed him by. A temple assistant walked over and looked at him lying there, but he also passed by on the other side."

✝ *17th August*

Would you make a decision about someone based on their appearance or their actions? These desperate, homeless children of Mine, will not attract you to them unless you have My heart. You must look beyond their dishevelled appearance, the dirt and the smell. There will be a mother somewhere who is grieving for them, just as I grieve for My lost sheep.

Care for the homeless as if they were your own children. A kind smile of understanding can warm the heart of the rejected. I love all My children equally, including the lost and lonely - people who need you, My child, to help them. Pray for their spiritual deliverance, but feed their tummies and wash their feet.

Luke 10:34-35

"Kneeling besides him the Samaritan soothed his wounds with medicine and bandaged them. Then he put the man on his own donkey and took him to an inn, where he took care of him."

✝ *18th August*

I love to see you as joyful and excited, as a basketful of kittens, discovering the world for the first time. Come and learn about new things with Me. Don't limit yourself in a mundane, repetitive religion. I want your walk with Me to be fresh and exciting. Try different churches until there is one that uplifts your spirit. When you enter through the doors, I want you to feel that you have come home.

Unless the spiritual home that you belong to is a place of sanctuary, joy and natural worship - a place which embraces everyone who seeks Me, then it could be the wrong place for you? Churches shouldn't be 'just' buildings, they should be inspiring places of love, that call to you and teach you and show My heart to everyone!

Hebrews 13:15-17

"With Jesus help, let us continually offer our sacrifice
of praise to God by proclaiming the glory of His name.
Don't forget to do good and to share what you have with
those in need, for such sacrifices are pleasing to God. Obey
your spiritual leaders and do what they say. Their work
is to watch over your souls and they are accountable to
God. Give them reason to do this joyfully and not with
sorrow."

✝ *19th August*

Have you taken stock recently, of all the things you have to be thankful for? When you feel grateful, My child, it pleases Me. You have much to celebrate; you have achieved success in many areas of your life, so don't take them for granted. Don't wait for the new year, to look back at all the joyful things in your life. Your ongoing appreciation will keep you humble.

Come before Me with thanks and praise, let Me share in your accomplishments. When you feel empowered by events, keep your feet firmly on the ground and let them help you to develop more trust in Me. If you keep Me at the centre of your life, you will remain grounded. There is no limit then, as to what you can achieve.

Colossians 2:7

"...Let your lives overflow with thanksgiving for all he has done."

✝ 20th August

I endeavour to lead you, but I am unable to when you shut Me out. Remind yourself how hard things get without Me. Pride comes before destruction, so don't let that be a reality in your life. What has changed to make you feel self-contained and capable of relying on yourself? Why have you moved away from Me? Are you alright on your own?

My everlasting arms are open wide, ready to support you. Turn away from your self-sufficiency, don't be sucked in by this immoral, corruptible, world. Those materialistic avenues are dead ends, to Christian values. Refuse to be led by the expectations of others. Talk to Me - I miss you.

Job 36:5-8

"God is mighty, yet he does not despise anyone! He is mighty in both power and understanding. He does not let the wicked live but gives justice to the afflicted. His eyes never leave the innocent, but he establishes and exhausts them with kings forever."

✝ *21st August*

The desert is a hot and lonely place. Are you happy wandering in the wilderness? No problem is too great for My attention. Bring everything that you are worried about and I will part the Red Sea. I know you're not happy in this destructive place, what has happened to cause us this separation? Don't ignore what you know to be My voice. I have been silent long enough.

Shutting yourself off from Me will cause your heart to decay. Confession will open a clear channel to Me again. Are you so drawn in by your new desires that I have become unimportant? I am here, My child - I have not moved away, but you have. Allow Me to help your suffering heart and to soothe your tired spirit. Nothing that has happened can separate you from My love.

Ezekiel 14:7

"I the Lord, will punish all those, both Israelites and foreigners, who reject me and set up idols in their hearts so they fall into sin."

✝ *22nd August*

Before you pray for My protection, make sure you are living in obedience to My will. Disobedience brings consequences. Sometimes your prayers show an immaturity. When you request My intervention even though you know that you are doing wrong, what response would you expect from me? If I allowed you to escape without teaching you anything, then what will prevent you from repeating the same action?

You teach your own children by laying down boundaries. I also have given you boundaries with My commandments. Abiding by these rules will keep you safe and build you into upstanding adults. My Word is a moral code on how you should live. Don't try to manipulate My love for you, by pushing the boundaries. Don't paint grey areas over what should remain black or white.

Hebrews 12:25

"See to it that you obey God, the one who is speaking to you. For if the people of Israel did not escape when they refused to listen to Moses, the earthy messenger, how terrible our danger, if we reject the one who speaks to us from heaven!"

✝ 23rd August

Your loving heart pleases Me. I have planted you among a rich variety of people, so don't be afraid of showing them you belong to Me. Live wisely in the midst of those who are not Christians. Unbelievers will watch your every move, especially during trying times, when you are required to show your moral strength. Tread very carefully, My child, and guard your tongue each time you speak.

Your kind actions will give you opportunities of showing My character, even if you utter no words. When others see your selfless acts of compassion, they will take note that you are different, and that the difference is that you know Me. Gradually doors will open and you will be credited with being a child of Mine.

1 Thessalonians 4:1

> *"Finally 'We urge you in the name of the Lord Jesus to live in a way that pleases God ... You are doing this already, and we encourage you to do so more and more.'"*

✝ *24th August*

The young foxes' russet coats gleam in the sunlight. Their troubles are far away as they enjoy full tummies. Many of My children are not so fortunate. The power struggles, in this troubled world, have made many refugees. Governments are corrupt and some take what is not theirs to have.

The innocent are at great risk for their lives. Don't be too at ease in this rich society. Don't let your comfortable circumstances reflect a satisfaction that cares little for their plight. Offer all you can, My child, and never miss an opportunity to help in any way possible that is within your capabilities.

Proverbs 28:27

"Whoever gives to the poor will lack nothing. But a curse will come on those who close their eyes to poverty."

✝ *25th August*

You know how hard it is to live a blameless life, yet that is what I ask of you. You understand the attitude and behaviour that is required by My code. Put yourself above the conflicts in your daily routine. Be ever listening to My Spirit who will make you conscious of 'easy sin' - that which you consider small such as white lies, hidden thoughts and actions.

Don't start to give in to have a quiet life. It is a slippery slope if you allow these sins to go unchecked, it will leave the door open for more. You have seen a coffee stain spread - it creeps stealthily, covering all it touches - sin is like that. Temptation is very real in your life and I see the daily battles you have. Combat those fights with thanksgiving and let Me strengthen you.

Romans 7:21-23

"It seems to be a fact of life that when I want to do what is right, I inevitably do what is wrong. I love God's law with all my heart. But there is another law at work within me that is at war with my mind. This law wins the fight and makes me a slave to the sin that is still within me."

✝ *26th August*

It is My law that reveals your sin; without it, you would be unaware of any wrongdoing. Even though you have given your life to Me, your old nature still exists and you are struggling. If you do what you want, especially at the expense of others, you will have no peace. Always that inner voice will be a nagging reminder.

Listen to My Spirit, as I long to set you on the right road. The world will continually challenge you. A large percentage of people don't follow My laws, even if they profess to be Christians. The path is rugged and many boulders will be in your way, but don't sit down and rest on them, rather climb over. I have supplied you with the resources to do this.

Romans 8:5-6

"Those who are dominated by the sinful nature think about sinful things, but those who are controlled by the Holy Spirit think about things that please the spirit. If your sinful nature controls your mind, there is death. But if the Holy Spirit controls your mind, there is life and peace."

✝ 27th August

Don't you find new life exciting, in all its forms, but especially the miracle of the birth of a baby? Take time to consider the process. Nine short months and another little soul can enter the world - perfect in form and function, able to breath and cry, wriggle and grasp, such a dependent little person. A loving family proudly leans over the cot, grinning, in overwhelming happiness.

Not all babies are warmly welcomed. Some are plummeted from the safety of the womb into a cold, hostile world. Some parents view them as an encumbrance. Their cries go unattended, they face neglect of the most dreadful kind. What of those tiny, helpless little ones with families who abuse them? Be vigilant and act quickly and help before it's too late.

Isaiah 49:15-16

> *"Never! Can a mother forget her nursing child? Can she feel no love for a child she has borne? But even if that were possible, I would not forget you! See I have written your name on my hand."*

✝ 28th August

Value your relationships because you don't know when you may lose them. Don't live with regrets, use every moment being conscious of how your actions are affecting others. Tolerate everyone, regardless of how they treat you. In this world of selfish motives, I want you to shine My light before you.

I know the effort it takes to overlook bad behaviour from someone else. You must continue to represent Me in all of your actions and responses. You can open doors for Me when you turn the other cheek and when you love despite being hurt. Let Me be the judge of those situations and just keep on reacting well in My presence.

Prayer

Father, when I am treated unfairly, help me not to return the same treatment. Help me to view all my friendships or acquaintances, with respect and a humble acceptance. Give me the grace to accept people as they are, without judgment. Make me a peacemaker. Amen.

✝ *29th August*

Is there someone in your life that you are being unfair to - someone you once loved desperately but have now discarded? Be careful, My child, the grass is not 'greener on the other side'. Be thankful for what you have and look for the good that is always present in you all. Life with the same person can become mundane, but you have the 'ability' to change your attitude towards that person.

Don't look at faults and find petty things to be discontented about. Don't compare your situation with that of someone else. You don't follow others home and see what goes on behind closed doors. No close relationship will be perfect. You must work at it and work at it some more. Be prepared to see both sides and never apportion blame. Arguments are never one-sided.

Ephesians 3:2-3

"Be humble and gentle. Be patient with each other, making allowance for each other's faults because of your love. Always keep yourself united in the Holy Spirit, and bind yourselves together in peace."

✝ *30th August*

From your conception when I formed you, I have planned your life. I have loved you from that moment. I will always love you. You are unique, special and extremely precious to Me. I will care for you no matter which road you chose to go down. The obstacles that you will encounter, are there to strengthen you. Never feel alone, My child, I am always there with you.

Just as I was in the cloud that the Israelites followed, so I hover over, around and in you. Even the tiniest emotion you feel, is of importance to Me. Trust that I always want the best for you and when you face trials, I am ready to guide your steps through them. You are of paramount importance to Me - please believe that. Share your innermost thoughts with Me, but don't forget to share the joy as well.

Isaiah 46:4

"I will be your God throughout you lifetime - until your hair is white with age. I made you, and I will care for you. I will carry you along and save you."

✝ *31st August*

This season is coming to an end and I am ready to move you onto a new thing. Your patience and endurance have been a worthwhile experience for you and will fortify you for what is to come. I never allow events in your life to occur, without first guiding their direction. The response you have is important to Me and can steer a different course to the one I intended.

The wind changes are unique to your life and together we will use them to prosper you. Look forward to the unexpected, because it will create a new opportunity for you - one that we will enjoy together. If you listen avidly to My call, you will enjoy the journey. Interruptions can be worked into My plan and become helpful, as I continually reform the way you are going and work it out for good.

Isaiah 42:1

"Look at my servant whom I strengthen. He is my chosen one, and I am pleased with him. I have put my spirit upon him."

September

✝ 1st September

The fruit of your character is shown in your conduct. The way you behave shows whether you are a child of Mine. It emphasises 'My image' in you. What would you like people to feel, after spending some time with you? I want them to feel the same way that you feel after spending some time in My company.

Your walk with Me is changing your character, little by little. You may think it is indiscernible, but those around you are benefitting, from the changes I am making within you. You are still a unique personality, but I have added a gentle heart of compassion. You are becoming more receptive to My ways, but always you will remain an individual I can enjoy being with.

Proverbs 21:2-3

"People may think they are doing what is right, but the Lord examines the heart. The Lord is more pleased when we do what is just and right than when we give him sacrifices."

✝ *2nd September*

You should not complain when things go awry for you, if you have not heeded My warnings. Examine your motives, examine your desires, who is to blame? Did you search My Word for your direction? Did you prayerfully invite Me into your decision making? Did you go ahead and please yourself, regardless of My warnings?

Oh, My child, be thankful that I will forgive your contrite heart no matter what you have done. Please don't allot blame where none is due. Let us recognise your mess as a rebellion, a mistake, a sin. Jesus died in order for you to be forgiven, don't accept that lightly, but do accept it readily and we will begin again.

Prayer

> *Lord, thank you for Your ready forgiveness. Please sharpen my senses to be constantly listening for Your voice. I ask for Your advice and then am attuned to the prompting of the Holy Spirit in warning me of the danger of imminent temptation. Help me to realise that You do tell me what's right, and it's I, who make the wrong choices. Amen*

✝ 3rd September

Be careful, My child, when things go well and you have great feelings of elation, it is at such times that the door can be opened for Satan. Don't drop your guard for a second. Pride can allow him access. When you have experienced victory in some area of your life and your spirit has soared, be aware that you are then most vulnerable to fatigue and discouragement.

Life is a cycle of ups and downs. After your 'spiritual highs' in particular, you will be under attack in order to spoil your success. Do not be led into feelings of depression; be aware that the enemy will use many tactics to bring you low. Hold onto the joy that your experience has caused you and remember that I still have a purpose in mind and My good purpose for you will be fulfilled.

1 Peter 5:8-9

"Be careful! Watch out for attacks from the Devil, your great enemy. He prowls around like a roaring lion, looking for some victim to devour. Take a firm stand against him and be strong in your faith."

✝ *4th September*

Do you really hold Me responsible for the things that regularly go wrong in your life? If they occur with monotonous regularity, you need to examine yourself, in order to determine who, if anyone, is to blame. Your choices are very often responsible for bad things that happen. They may not be choices that you should have made.

But what happens next, will be your choice. How you choose to deal with things - whether an apology is the answer or whether it is a lesson you have learnt. Whatever the scenario, involve Me. I can ease your burdens, I see the wider picture and I will give you My wisdom in order to find the solution.

Proverbs 24:3-4

> *"A house is built by wisdom and becomes strong through good sense. Through knowledge its rooms are filled with all sorts of precious riches and valuables."*

✝ 5th September

I want you to learn the deeper things of Me. Does your trust plummet when you think I have let you down, or do you look for a lesson? I can protect you from all downfalls, but if I did that, would you then just treat Me as a magic formula? Do you not think your trust would, in the long run, suffer? I am gratified, by My children who believe in Me no matter what befalls them.

When you have reached a low point in this life, it is then, My child, that you will realise I am all you really need. This kind of trust has no conditions and leaves Me the freedom to truly lead you. All the barriers are removed, your heart is openly exposed to Me and it is then that I can work in your situation.

Colossians 1:13

"For he has rescued us from the one who rules in the kingdom of darkness, and has brought us into the kingdom of his dear son."

✝ 6th September

The evil consequences for your soul, are right here, now, not up ahead in the future! Time is shorter than you could ever imagine and I want you to pursue Me with urgency. You would not walk past a sign that said 'Danger' because your common sense would alert you to a hazard.

But by walking on the edge of My Word, you are risking harm to your soul. I have forgiven your sins, but that doesn't mean you can live your life in disregard to My teaching. Heed the warning signs and return to Me.

2 Peter 2:9

"So you see the Lord knows how to rescue godly people from their trials, even while punishing the wicked right up until the day of judgement."

✝ 7th September

False witnesses are already in the world. My child, be on your guard as they will sweeten their words and will seem to make so much sense. Go back to your Bible and the very real warnings are there, against these eloquent speakers. Some have had experience of Me and have lost their way.

Beware of their plausible arguments. Their words are destructive and Satan has a stealthy way of invading your mind. Only by your close, personal relationship with Me, am I able to protect you. Search out the truth in My Word and believe what I say. I will penetrate your heart when you search for Me.

2 Peter 2:1

"But there were also false prophets in Israel, just as there will be false teachers among you. They will cleverly teach their destructive heresies about God and even turn against their master who brought them. Theirs will be a swift and terrible end."

✝ *8th September*

There are many in this world who consider what I say is sin to be acceptable. Little by little, society has become more secular, and I am being removed. They appear to be gaining the upper hand. Human rights have prevented judgemental attitudes. Although they are correct in their place, they make My children too afraid to stand up for Me. You need to look inside yourself, and consider whether this is happening to you.

Don't go along with the things that My law clearly states are wrong. Make yourself familiar with what I tell you is sin! Be upright in your beliefs and in your actions. Your life must be lived with transparency.

John 15:18-19

> *"When the world hates you, remember it hated me before it hated you. The world would love you if you belonged to it. , but you don't. I chose you to come out of the world and so it hates you."*

✝ 9th September

Know for sure what you claim to believe, and make sure you can back up these claims with My Word. Study the areas that most concern you, and I will bring joy as you gain revelations. My child, you belong to Me and as a family member, you will share the joy of being My child with others. Listen with an uncritical ear to the views of others. Each of My children are at a different stage of discovery, so join together as you learn from one another.

My child, I have given you your own personal ministry - it is unlike any other. Grow in those strengths, but in a humble way. I love to see you sharing and supporting each other. Bring Me naturally into your conversations and I will clear the way for you to experience My presence.

Prayer

Lord, thank you that you place us with other like-minded Christians. Help us to talk freely about You with one another. Teach us that to pray together is the most natural thing in the world. Forgive our reticence to do that.
Amen.

✝ 10th September

When My Son left His disciples, He promised to return in the presence of the Holy Spirit. As a man, He was limited to being in one place, but the Holy Spirit is able to live in all the hearts of those who are saved. That promise is open to all who believe that Jesus is My Son and died for them in order for their sins to be forgiven.

That promise is open to you today!

John 14:23-26

"Jesus said, 'All those who love me will do what I say. My father will love them and we will come to them and live in them. Anyone who doesn't love me will not do what I say. And remember my words are not my own. This message is from the father who sent me. I am telling you these things now, while I am still with you. But when the father sends the counsellor as my representative and by the counsellor, I mean the Holy Spirit - he will teach you everything and remind you of everything I myself have told you.' "

✝ 11th September

Come to Me when your fear threatens to overtake you. The immediate, unknown future, can be very frightening. Events are unfolding at an alarming rate, but all these things that terrify you, must come to pass. Look to Me for encouragement; I see the horrors of terrorism all over the world.

These are dreadful, random acts of violence which are beyond justification. Many seem to have an unknown source and therefore they become even more terrifying; when the outcome is fear without reason and understanding, it may seem you are fighting an unseen enemy. Allow Me to ease the panic and strengthen you. I am with you forever!

Psalm 46:1-3

"God is our refuge and strength, always ready to help in times of trouble. So we will not fear, even if earthquakes come and the mountains crumble into the sea."

✝ *12th September*

I am a merciful God. I have allowed My people time to repent and seek forgiveness. I am merciful but I cannot tolerate sin. A time is coming when the wicked who have consistently turned away from Me, will receive justice for their iniquities. The world asks how some of My people behave in evil ways and yet seem to escape punishment. It will not always be so.

Look to your owns deeds not those of someone else. Do all you can to help one another stay on the narrow path, but you can't be responsible for other peoples' actions. A time is coming when everyone will have had the opportunity to hear about the sacrifice that Jesus made. It is not until then that I will judge the world.

Matthew 24:21-22

"For that will be a time of greater horror than anything the world has ever seen or will ever see again. In fact unless that time of calamity is shortened, the entire human race will be destroyed. But it will be shortened because of God's chosen ones."

✝ 13th September

When your heart is full of sadness, remember Me. You must try to think positive thoughts about your situation. Do you know that you can think positively, even though your mind is screaming the opposite? Cling to what you know - My promises - and take courage from My presence. I will always be with you, even during times of adversity when you seem to think that I am absent.

Once I am invited into your life I will be with you in all your trials. My Spirit will support and uplift you. Looking back, you will see where I was. Put your hand into Mine and lean your full weight upon Me. Confess to Me your fear, your grief and your worries. Don't be tentative when including Me. Claim the promises I have made to you and wait patiently for My intervention.

Hebrews 13:5-6

"... 'I will never fail you. I will never forsake you.' That is why we can say with confidence, the Lord is my helper, so I will not be afraid, what can mere mortals do to me?"

✝ 14th September

Your life is a gift from Me. If you are dissatisfied, you will find it hard to look on it as a gift. Do you see more negative things than positive? Do you have more problems than you feel able to deal with? Are they too numerous to mention? The flaws are not in My plan and they don't come from Me! Your reaction to adversity can emphasise the things that you find difficult.

Your attitude can build or destroy. Take a long look at your life and let Me help you to start again, resolving one problem at a time. Together we can conquer them and they will seem as nothing. As you overcome, be ready to help someone else who is experiencing something similar. Kindness and true empathy will help you and those to whom you show it.

Romans 12:2

"Don't copy the behaviour and customs of this world, but let God transform you into a new person by changing the way you think. Then you will know what God wants you to do, and you will know how good and pleasing and perfect his will really is."

✝ *15th September*

Look closely at the things that distress you. Where does the distress come from? Your feelings of inadequacy, or an outcome you didn't expect? Have you deliberately gone your own way, forgetting My teaching? Examine your deeds very carefully; it is easy for you to want something so badly, that it takes precedence over everything else, especially My laws and your common sense.

I understand your human frailties. My Spirit is gentle and will only nudge you quietly. Though you have free will, wrong thoughts can colour your decisions. If your disappointments come regardless of your obedience, then trust that I have a better plan in place. My child, your heart is very fragile and I have it safely in My care. Trust Me.

Psalm 33:20

"We depend on the Lord alone to save us. Only he can help us, protecting us like a shield."

✝ *16th September*

Do you think I have failed to answer a prayer? Is that why you are distant and upset, or is there more to it? My child, do you think I would fail you? Can I refer you back to My promises! Your brooding will allow your emotions to get the better of you and Satan will take control. His whisperings are false!

I want you to examine your feelings and realise how far from the truth they are. I want what is best for you in all things. Don't mistake My lack of response to your call, for My ignoring it. Don't rush in and try to solve your problem without Me. I can hear you, I know what's best for you and trusting Me with patience and endurance will bring its rewards.

2 Corinthians 4:18

> *"So we don't look at the troubles we can see right now;*
> *rather we look forward to what we have not yet seen. For*
> *the troubles we see will soon be over, but the joys to come*
> *will last forever."*

✝ *17th September*

My child, do you know there is such a thing as the sin of omission? As you grow closer to Me and learn to let My Word sink deeper into your soul, you will come to understand this. Sin isn't always something you have done; there is much sin in My people as a result of the things they have failed to do.

Each step with Me is a trained path; that's why it is called the narrow road. Your conscience is a deep, complicated area. I will help you to listen attentively and I will supply you with the grace to affirm and then act on what My Spirit tells you to do.

James 4:17

"Remember it is a sin to know what you ought to do and then not do it."

✝ 18th September

When I look at you, My child, I see your beauty, and I see you as you are - righteous in My Son. I see the changed person you will become - when My work will be completed in you. I don't see what man sees, I cannot look at you in sin. The blood of Jesus has washed you absolutely clean. His goodness radiates from you.

One day you will understand how His sacred act of crucifixion has provided you with a future. No amount of good deeds can make you worthy, but His blood has given you a name - 'child of God.' My child, you are a blessing to all of My church. Work together with My other children and love one another into My Kingdom.

Prayer

Father, I can never repay the huge debt that I owe Jesus, so help me never to undervalue it. It is beyond my comprehension to love unconditionally, but I want to try and live that way. Help me to change daily, from the inside out, until I am what You want me to be. Amen.

✝ 19th September

I offer a compassionate heart that will hold the truth in love. Be wary of hurting one another by brutal honesty, but be prepared to tell the truth with a sensitive heart. Give up your false lifestyles and be a person of integrity who will honour My name. Be kind to those who ask your opinion - but don't really want the truth.

Don't always hide behind a facade of niceness, if the truth can save one of your brothers or sisters from a mistake, then you must voice it. Equally don't force your views; if uninvited, then you should remain silent. Above all, continue in love with consideration for truth. Do not deliberately hurt your neighbour, or agree when you know that something is wrong.

Ephesians 4:15

"Instead we will hold to the truth in love, becoming more and more in every way like Christ, who is the head of his body the church."

✝ *20th September*

I gave you the capacity for desire and I can prompt your desires to be right with Me. I gave you the capacity to hunger and thirst, and I can direct those hungers to come under your self-control. I will empower you to have healthy desires. I offer you a new life - a life that's full of victory.

I have put My Spirit in you and My strength will enable you to accomplish things that you never imagined possible. If you truly want to follow Me, I will develop your gifts and remove all the obstructions that are holding you back.

Ezekiel 36:35

"And when I bring you back, people will say, "This godforsaken land is now like Eden's garden."

✝ *21st September*

Examine the world I have created and just take time to revel in the wonder of it. How many times do you walk past the beauty that is all around you? You soak up the warmth of the sunshine and enjoy its wonderful benefits, but do you take all of them for granted?

Look at the vastness and power of the ocean. Feel the sand between your toes and the coolness of the water lapping against the rocks. Let your senses take in the vessel gliding on the calm sea; the distant cry of the seagull, and its precision as it dives, coming up with a fish in its beak. Absorb the excited screams of the little ones, jumping on their newly-built sand castle; My donkeys with their tinkling bells, giving rides as one once did for Jesus. I created all these things for your enjoyment and it gives Me pleasure when you notice.

Genesis 1:1-3

"In the beginning God created the earth. The earth was empty, a formless mass cloaked in darkness. And the spirit of God was hovering over the surface."

✝ *22nd September*

Do you believe the misconception of My creation being an accidental event or an uncontrolled explosion? Can anything in this world be something that has just occurred, without any planning and design?

Your logic must tell you that this cannot be! Consider the complexities of each area of creation; nothing that is so intricate in its construction could have happened without a superior inventor. I am your God, Creator of all things.

Thought

> *The documented story of God's creation in Genesis has been dismissed as a fairy tale for too long. Evolution has no foundation in science and is based on observation. Darwin's theory that human beings developed from apes, has no fossilised evidence, in fact there is no evidence at all. Why, if there were any truth in it, do we not find any evolution going on today?*

✝ *23rd September*

Have you ever considered the complex workings of the human eye? Can those intricate workings be explained by evolution? You have a natural tendency to want to know the answers. Why not search My Word with the leading of My Spirit and you 'will' discover the true meaning of life.

How blessed are My children who look and find themselves and believe what My Spirit tells them. Don't get too hung up on things you don't understand. At the proper time, when you are spiritually ready, these powerful truths will be revealed to you. For now, trust Me.

1 Corinthians 2:13-14

"When we tell you this, we do not use words of human wisdom. We speak words given to us by the spirit, using the spirits words to explain spiritual truths. But people who aren't Christians can't understand these truths from God's spirit. It all sounds foolish to them because only those who have the spirit can understand what the spirit means."

✝ *24th September*

My Spirit is eager to lead you. Begin each day by first being thankful. This will cleanse your thoughts, then ask that My Spirit will lead you. Surrender all your decisions, invite Me into each step of this day. Watch as I work out the best for you, see the tensions recede as you learn to rely on Me.

Nothing that concerns you is too mundane a concern for Me. I love to share the little things that build up the picture of your life. If you listen closely to Me, I will bring you early warnings. Don't allow these warnings to distress you, they are meant for your good. Heed that uneasy feeling you get about something, and ask if it comes from Me.

Romans 8:14

"For all who are led by the spirit of God, are children of God. So you should not be like cowering slaves. You should behave instead like God's very own children, adopted into his family - calling him father, dear father."

✝ 25th September

You are part of My family and I want you to love your extended family, the church, as they are My people. Try to maintain a strong sense of belonging. There is a worldwide circle of My family. Don't find yourself in an insular pocket that looks in on itself. Expand your horizons to embrace all of My children.

Include those who don't yet know Me, that they can be 'born again', into this loving family unit. They especially need you to love them. There are lost souls that are searching in their hearts which tell them - "There must be more than this." Be ready to show them what it is.

1 John 3:1

"See how very much our father loves us, for he allows us to be called his children, and we really are! But the people who belong to this world don't know God, so they don't understand that we are his children."

✝ *26th September*

I love to see your enjoyment, especially in the natural world. The excitement I see in you, as you crunch your way through the russet Autumn leaves. The sun is losing its hot warmth as it kisses goodbye to summer. But as you tidy up the garden and prepare the ground, be ready to plant for next season.

Don't let your heart grow cold to the beauty that is still all around you. Gather in the crops and be grateful for the harvest. Allow My gifts of good things to sustain you. Share all My blessings with a thankful heart. Don't allow the end of a season to prevent you from continuing to gather.

Proverbs 14:4

> *"Where there are no oxen, the manger is empty, but from the strength of an ox comes an abundant harvest.*

✝ *27th September*

Do you know you can choose love or hate, joy or misery? Who, My child, would want the latter? In all things, you can adopt a right attitude. I want you to nurture the fruits of goodness, deep within your heart, and allow their shoots to come forward and take up root in all those whom they touch.

By your having a consistently right reaction, especially during adversity, you will express more to people about Me than you could possibly imagine. They will see My strength, working to support you, and your calmness and acceptance will teach them about My grace.

Psalm 45:7

You love what is right and hate what is wrong. Therefore God, your God - has anointed you, pouring out the oil of joy on you more than anyone else.

✝ *28th September*

I miss you, My child, when your life becomes too intense for you to spend meaningful time with Me. How much rushing about you do! Can you remember how you felt yesterday? Did your mind entertain any thoughts of Me? Or were you so engrossed that I wasn't included?

Don't delay our time together for too long. The danger will come if you leave an empty space in your life, that ought to be filled by Me. It is a slippery slope when you allow all the many emotions you feel, to crowd out all thoughts of Me. Remember Me, My child.

Prayer

Father, I have allowed my life to become too busy and thus have neglected You. I suffer for Your perceived absence and I'm sorry. Please enable me to manage my time better and to put You 'first' each day, before I develop a habit of leaving you until last. Amen.

✝ 29th September

Are you afraid of circumstances that you feel are beyond your control? Are you facing a series of choices that make you afraid of the outcome? Often your decisions will have a moral issue attached and you must weigh up your options, without worrying too much about the outcome becoming one you would regret.

Are you more worried about your popularity, loss of comfort, or even worse. Don't hesitate to do what you know is morally right. Don't allow the devil to threaten your soul. The key question is - are you going to listen to My Spirit?

Proverbs 2:6-7

"For the Lord grants wisdom! From his mouth come knowledge and understanding. He grants a treasure of good sense to the a godly. He is their shield protecting those who walk with integrity."

✝ *30th September*

My child, look ahead with your hand in Mine and leave all your worries with Me. I will protect you from the forces in this world that seek to steal you from Me. Place all those you hold dear into My loving care and believe that My goodness will surround them.

Release the storms of emotion into My unlimited compassion and I will use them to empower you. Break down the strongholds that separate you from Me by giving over your control. Unless I am invited into your heart to have free reign, I will not intervene. But once I'm invited, sit back and watch, as I calm the storm and bring peace.

Prayer

Father, thank you that in my heart I know You love me and want to solve my problems. Increase my trust to truly give all my worries to You and know that You will solve them in the best way for me. Give me patience to wait on Your timing and not follow my contingency plan. In Jesus' name. Amen.

October

 *1st October*

You will have to experience trials in your life which I will use to refine you. They are life's experiences. Everyone, Christian or not, will have trials - it is the cycle of everyday life. The difference is how you react, and ultimately cope with them.

There was no promise of an easy ride when you invited Me into your life, but you have the promise of My help throughout those times of adversity. It is your attitude that strengthens your character and ultimately your faith.

Prayer

Father, forgive me when I have a wrong attitude. Help me to bear adversity with a smile and in the power of Your Spirit. Thank you that You promise that I need never face anything alone. Amen.

✝ *2nd October*

Jesus said "My peace I leave with you ..." Do you know that you have My peace always available; it is down to you whether you embrace it. Believe that My promises, are sincere and true. I am always here waiting to comfort you. My peace will remove your worries, if not your problems.

I have supplied all you need in order for you to carry on your life with a joyful heart. It is a blessing that I give to you, My child. When others see your good attitude, in response to your hardships, they will see the difference that I make to your life.

John 14:27-29

> *"I am leaving you with a gift - peace of mind and heart.*
> *And the peace that I give isn't like the peace the world*
> *gives. So don't be troubled or afraid."*

✝ *3rd October*

Laughter is a good medicine and I long to hear you giggling. The things that you see on the news are distressing, but if you have done all you are able to do, within your own capabilities, then leave the rest in My hands. I have motivated those in high positions to make the necessary changes to laws, in governments, in charitable giving, aid workers - in fact, all who have listened.

Your compassion does you credit, but don't allow the cruelty and the occurrence of natural disasters to take over your thoughts. If you have truly done your part, then you must step away and allow Me to work. Do not feel guilty because of what you have. It is not given at the expense of someone else, but it can be shared by you, if you are willing.

1 John 3:18-20

"Dear children, let us stop just saying we love each other; let us really show it by our actions. It is by our actions that we know we are living in the truth, so we will be confident when we stand before the Lord. Even if our hearts condemn us. For God is greater than our hearts and he knows everything."

✝ 4th October

Sometimes you lose something in your life that devastates you. It is during these times that you have a fork in the road. Which way will you choose, My child? We can grow much closer, as you learn to trust and rely on Me more. If you choose the wrong path and leave Me behind, I will remain with you. I will patiently wait for an invitation to be included in your life again.

I see what is at the end of each fork, you are required to go ahead in faith. Will you invite Me down the same road with you? Search the Scriptures and find one that comforts you and keep repeating the words over and over to yourself. My Word has power in it and I will add strength if you choose to rely on Me.

Joshua 1:8

"Study this book of the law continually. Meditate on it day and night so you may be sure to obey all that is written in it. Only then will you succeed."

✝ 5th October

As you mature in your walk with Me, you will start to feel comfortable and safe. Be careful with these feelings, especially during these times when you might become too relaxed in My comfort, as Satan will try to destroy what we are enjoying together. Look at My servant, Job.

Satan will bring temptations and try to undermine My communion with you. Put on My armour against these attacks and never be too complacent with your life. A time is coming when My closest servants will be tested in their faith to the extreme.

2 Corinthians 13:5-6

"Examine yourselves to see if your faith is really genuine. Test yourselves. If you cannot tell that Jesus Christ is among you, it means you have failed the test. I hope you recognise that we have passed the test and are approved by God."

✝ *6th October*

Wake up, My child, and realise how the things that are occurring, were predicted. The birth pains have begun in earnest. All that you see happening in the world, is terrifying. Be courageous and continue to follow Me. Don't allow outside influences to sway your resolve.

You have My love - it is the strongest bond there is. No matter how much the world is trying to break it, nothing is more important to Me than My care for you. Hold onto to My hand tightly and equip yourself with My word, ready for the fight.

Romans 10:17

"Yet faith comes from listening to this message of good news - the good news about Christ."

✝ 7th October

Don't be afraid when your circumstances change. The world is changing, but you are My child and you have the promise of salvation. You will be resurrected and live with Me in heaven forever! Jesus has taken all your sin and due suffering upon Himself; His sacrificial death was in your place!

Have no fear about the future. Nothing can separate you from Me, I will never allow Satan to steal you away from Me. Your courage will increase, your strength will gain momentum and all who see you, will acknowledge that you are My child!

Thought

God has given you power in the Holy Spirit. Draw on the strength that is given freely, since you can do nothing to earn it. Jesus is the way.

✝ 8th October

I will heal your brokenness. Surrender all that has hurt you, all that you have done to hurt someone else and all that you struggle to forgive. I know it's hard, My child; you have lived with so much heartache for so very long. Let us begin with the things that you have done.

Remember each one, beginning at your earliest memory. Bring it to mind and lay it out before Me. Don't hold onto anything. You have buried so much, that it has become a part of you. These distressing memories are preventing your cleansing from being complete. Let Me in, My child!

Ephesians 5:5

"You can be sure that no immoral, impure, or greedy person will inherit the Kingdom of Christ and of God."

✝ *9th October*

Now, My child, open up those deeply buried secrets to Me - things that are too painful for you to talk about, the hurts that have caused you lasting damage. Unless they are revealed and brought into the light, how can you truly let them go? You must make a determined effort to speak about your distress to Me.

It may take you many attempts, My child. I am patient, we will continue at your speed. A wound takes time to heal. It must first be exposed, cleaned, and left open to My Spirit, to begin the healing process. Trust Me to remove the rot that is causing your joy to decay.

Ephesians 5:6-9

"Don't be fooled by those who try to excuse these sins, for the terrible anger of God comes upon all those who disobey him. Don't participate in the things these people do. For though your hearts were once full of darkness, now you are full of light from the Lord, and your behaviour should show it. For this light within you produces only what is good and right and pure."

✝ *10th October*

Make a stance, My child, against anything that you know is not right. Protect the little ones from any exposure to things that will damage them. The culture of this world is breeding lethargy about some dangerous issues.

People are allowing the 'anything goes' motto to become rife in schools, public places, on TV, anywhere that is aimed at the children. Corruption is rife and crime is a usual headline. It is not acceptable. Jesus didn't die for the world to become a den of iniquity. Turn away and stand strong against this evil, My child.

Ephesians 5:11-14

> *"Take no part in the worthless deeds of evil and darkness; instead, rebuke and expose them. It is shameful even to talk about the things that ungodly people do in secret. But when the light shines on them, it becomes clear how evil these things are. And where your light shines it will expose their evil deeds."*

✝ *11th October*

Thank Me for the prayers of My people. If you could count them, you would be astounded. I hear each one, there is a beautiful aroma in heaven from the Holy Spirit's interpretation of each word. Sometimes you find talking to Me is difficult and there are many reasons for that. Please try and put aside the obstructions which are of your making.

Come readily into My presence and explain what is wrong and what you need from Me. I am a tolerant Father, slow to anger and I will always be patient and listening. All your problems, which are huge to you, are just small blips to Me, and easily addressed, if only you bring them to Me readily and wait patiently for answers.

Isaiah 30:18

"But the Lord still waits for you to come to him so he can show you his love and compassion. For the Lord is a faithful God. Blessed are those who wait for him to help them."

✝ *12th October*

Don't be disappointed when things don't go as you would like them to. Your prayers need to be confidently handed over to Me. I will always examine them with due consideration. Some will be answered positively, with speed, and this will give you encouragement.

My child, you must accept My decision; it will be one that is in your best interest. 'No' doesn't necessarily mean 'never', it could mean 'wait'. But whatever the answer is, you can be assured that I know and act on what is the right thing for you. Your prayers will be granted when you pray in line with My will.

Hebrews 10:19-20

"And so dear brothers and sisters, we can boldly enter heaven's Most Holy Place because of the blood of Jesus. This is the new life giving way that Christ has opened up for us through the sacred curtain, by means of his death for us."

✝ *13th October*

The Autumn months, which signify an end to the Summer, are a time to gather in the harvest, put away the things used in the warm season and tidy up, in preparation for the barren months ahead. What has been accomplished over the year? Have you used every opportunity, or do you have regrets?

Don't wallow in what might have been, or mistakes you have made. Take the experiences and make use of them. Any crop that has failed must not be planted again. Remember the areas where the seedlings grew expertly, weed and develop these. Be ruthless in clearing out that which you won't need again. Don't hold on to things that are worthless.

John 15:4

"Remain in me and I will remain in you. For a branch cannot produce fruit if it is severed from the vine, and you cannot be fruitful apart from me."

✝ *14th October*

Your trust in Me is one of the most valued attributes of our walk. The scale of this trust is coloured by past experiences. You need to truly acknowledge Me and My plans for you, as being what is best for you.

Our journey together should be viewed as an adventure into unknown territory, and one that you are determined to enjoy; you will, if you learn complete trust in Me. I will act above and beyond your expectations. I am in control, but you need to surrender your will to Me. Trust Me that I have a plan.

Zephaniah 3:17

"For the Lord your God has arrived to live among you. He is a mighty saviour. He will rejoice over you with great gladness. With His love, He will calm all your fears. He will exult over you by singing a happy song."

✝ *15th October*

Let go of your plans for your life, long enough to examine Mine. I want you to be happy and I will never force My will upon you. I will not bulldoze you into following My plan, unless your choice holds danger for you; it is then that My Spirit will warn you.

You will, through your faith, begin to see that My direction for your life is a good one. Even your own ideas can be woven into Mine. It's what makes our life together exciting - because of your individuality.

John 15:11

> *"I have told you this so that you will be filled with joy.*
> *Yes your joy will overflow."*

✝ *16th October*

My Son died for you, whilst you were still sinful. Imagine doing something for another out of love, knowing that they may be totally unappreciative. Then imagine all the pain, humiliation and the horrific death that Jesus agreed to suffer, on your behalf.

Imagine being born into this world, leaving your crown behind, with the knowledge that you would be put to death, in the most barbaric way. Jesus did it for you, My child, and for the world who have rejected Him. Help those who don't know what this rejection means. Time is short, My child.

Luke 23:34

"And Jesus said, 'Father forgive them for they don't know what they do.'"

✝ *17th October*

The greatest 'power of darkness' that the world has ever seen is soon to be unleashed. Sodom and Gomorrah was only a taster for the way things are today. I brought destruction upon them. A time is coming when the sun will darken. Be ever vigilant and on your guard so that your foot won't slip.

Jesus is fighting for those souls which are stubborn; they have heard the Word and still they won't surrender. Are you prepared for the fight? Are you a Christian soldier? When all of the people in the world have heard the message, Jesus will return! Will you be ready?

Matthew 25:10

"But while they were gone to buy oil, the bridegroom came, and those who were ready went in with him, to the marriage feast, and the door was locked."

✝ *18th October*

Learn scriptures, My child, so that you are armed with a necessary response during troubled times. There is power in My Word. You will discover the meaning of life, the road will become a route of clear signs. The direction that is meant for you will open up in a victorious parade of brightness, that will help to focus your eyes.

Remain constant in the search that brings life. It's a unique relationship with Me. Savour our time together, repel all outside distractions, and prevent anything that would seek to interfere or come between us. Behold all that I am and all that you are becoming in My name.

Prayer

Father, I know that I am nothing without You. Thank you that now I am righteous in Christ. Thank you for showing me the way to true happiness and contentment. Empower me to learn deeply the meaning of Your Word and to retain it. Amen.

✝ *19th October*

Sometimes in your effort to lead a good life, you become overly busy. This allows the channels between us to become blocked and get so cluttered with debris that My voice is muffled. Examine where you have allowed this overload to become an issue.

Ask Me and I will show you when you should say 'No'! If you start to make working for men your first priority, then our time together will suffer. At some stage, you will reach burnout. Make Me your first calling when you awaken. I will teach you to manage your time.

John 9:4

> *"All of us must quickly carry out the tasks assigned to us by the one who sent me, because there is little time left before the night falls and all work comes to an end."*

✝ *20th October*

Is there an area in which you need healing? I am the Father of all things! My first desire is for wholeness. I am the healing God, slow to anger and quick to forgive. Bring every niggle to Me, even those that you consider old age pains. Yes, your body will age, but the things I teach you can help it to age well.

If you have a serious, pressing complaint, bring it quickly to Me. If you allow Me access, I will address all of your needs, spiritual, emotional and physical. My timing is not yours. Be patient and wait with faithful expectancy. Remember though that anything I permit to remain, will be used by Me for your ultimate good.

Deuteronomy 7:15

"And the Lord will protect you from all sickness. He will not let you suffer from the terrible diseases you knew in Egypt, but He will bring them all on your enemies."

✝ 21st October

This generation is not unique in its desire for self-indulgence, nor its need for complete self-gratification. Happiness and fulfilment don't reign from such things. Honest wealth is a good thing, but many have reached where they are today through their selfish, dishonest activities. Prosperity is a gift from Me and needs to be shared.

There is a greedy misuse of money and you know that material things are but fleeting. Be honest in all your dealings and share with all who have less than you and are in need, with a heart of compassion. Prosperity if misused, is one of the greatest destroyers of your relationship with Me.

Matthew 6:31-33

> *"So don't worry about having enough food or drink or clothing. Why be like the pagans who are so deeply concerned about these things? Your Heavenly Father already knows your needs and he will give you all you need from day to day if you live for him and make the Kingdom of God your primary concern."*

✝ 22nd October

I see everything! Is there anything in your life that you would seek to hide from Me? If you have a contrite heart,there is nothing that I will not forgive. What in your life seems more important than Me? From the first time you became aware of Me, you have been in charge of your schedule.

Sometimes it feels that I need an appointment to spend time with you. I love to see all the activities that you are involved with, but not at the expense of our timetable together. You can list, in order of priority, all that is important to you. Pray over it and I will lead and help you to manage your days.

Jeremiah 2:32

"Does a young woman forget her jewellery? Does a bride hide her wedding dress? No! Yet for years on end people have forgotten me."

✝ 23rd October

You have many dimensions in this life. Don't compartmentalise Me. Just as My children are My priority, I want to be theirs. Do you understand how much easier every aspect of your life would become, if you consulted with Me first.

By spending time with Me, your processing of events, will be more successful. Let us prepare the day's plan together. If you are busy, you need to pray more! I can steer you away from unnecessary labour. My peace, in your plans, will lend wings to your feet.

James 1:17

"Whatever is good and perfect comes from to us from God above, who created all heaven's lights. Unlike them he never changes or casts shifting shadows."

✝ *24th October*

All your life you have had passions. These are the abilities that I have gifted to you. These gifts are to be nurtured for My Kingdom. Have you not noticed that some of the things you are capable of, seem simple to you but are difficult for others?

Although you are blessed in My family, all of you are achievers in different ways. Encourage each other in your varied gifts and be humble in yours. Express interest in each other and appreciation. I want harmony to reign within My church. Look upon each person as important.

Exodus 31:3

"I have filled him with the Spirit of God, giving him great wisdom, intelligence and skill in all kinds of craft."

✝ 25th October

The road to sin and corruption is laden with pleasures but they are very short-lived and lead to misery. The road to salvation is paved with the passion of My Son. Faith and trust lead to joy and a life spent with Jesus. Don't gratify your carnal desires with the world's worthless treasures.

All these elements are perishable. Clothe yourselves with compassion and sensitivity. Don't allow Satan to hold you captive to sin by which you will crumble and decay. Increase your joy by believing that Jesus died to set you free.

2 Peter 1:3

"As we know Jesus better, His divine power gives us everything we need for living a Godly life. He has called us to receive His own glory and goodness!"

✝ *26th October*

Your body is the temple of the Holy Spirit! It is the sacred shrine that He dwells in! You were purchased by the blood of Jesus and He sent My Spirit to live within your heart. His desire is to convey to you a new way of living your life; not by mindlessly obeying, but by His nurturing within you the fruits that characterise Jesus.

Honour the presence of The Holy Spirit. Welcome His input in your choices. You are redeemed. By dedicating your life to Me in all you do, you express to the world that you are My child.

Ephesians 4:30

> *"And do not bring sorrow to God's Holy Spirit by the way you live. Remember He is the One who has identified you as His own, guaranteeing that you will be saved on the day of redemption."*

✝ 27th October

Do not be afraid, the world might be currently controlled by Satan, but I am gathering My warriors around Me and a time of tribulation is coming. Satan seeks to discredit My church. He spreads lies and his persuasive ways are abominable.

Be ready to refute his actions. Be ready to ask for discernment, in order to recognise when a response from you is necessary. You are a new person inside, so you need to ask Me to provide My grace when it is necessary and when you need to stand up against adversity.

2 Corinthians 1:5

"You can be sure that the more we suffer for Christ, the more God will shower us with His comfort through Christ."

✝ *28th October*

Do you truly believe that I am always with you? Do you believe that I am there helping you to undertake every task? Blessed are My children who do. Nothing in your life is too lowly for My involvement. I am pleased if your faith is such that you are aware of My presence.

Look for Me in the garden, I love nature and you will find Me there. Walk with Me as Adam did; let us rest a while and chat. I enjoy your company, in the quiet of the day, before and after it is done.

Genesis 3:8-9

"Toward evening they heard the Lord God walking about in the garden, so they hid themselves among the trees. The Lord God called to Adam, 'where are you?' "

✝ *29th October*

You need to recognise the power and the cunning of the tempter. He and his cohorts are watching, biding their time, ready to trick you. The mind is an easy target; that is why you must soak yourself in My Word. The more readily the Scriptures come to mind, the bigger the defence you will have against Satan.

He comes in the night like a thief, to rob you of your peace. He will undermine your abilities by attacking your self-esteem. He will make you feel unsure, unworthy; don't mistake what he will tell you as the truth. Defend yourself by calling on the powerful name of Jesus.

Matthew 4:3-5

> *"Then the Devil came and said to Him, 'If you are the son of God, change these stones into loaves of bread.' But Jesus said, 'No, the scriptures says, people need more than bread for their life, they must feed on every word of God.'*
> "

✝ *30th October*

My child, you are achieving so much for Me. By wanting to live a worthy life in Christ, you choose not to live as the world does. I see all that you strive to do and it pleases Me. I am moulding the changes in you and I will never let you go. I will never be forceful, but because your heart is for Me, you are making My work easier.

Allow Me more of your time to carry on this process and continue to respond to Me with an open heart. Your thankful attitude allows Me quick access and I value your willingness to change. Place all that you offer before Me and I will use it and multiply your gifts.

Romans 12:3

"As God's messenger, I give each of you this warning; Be honest with yourselves, by measuring your value by how much faith God has given you."

✝ *31st October*

If you are fully committed to Me, you will truly love your brothers and sisters. That includes those who don't look like you, who aren't so particular, who behave differently, who haven't learnt about the niceties in life, or those who have mental health issues. How committed do you feel to loving them?

Can you honestly say you love them, enough to put your arms around them and make them feel special? I don't mean a fleeting trip to help, as that will only make you feel better. I mean caring day in day out for My children who are suffering, and those who are lost.

2 John 1:6

"Love means doing what God has commanded us and He has commanded us to love one another, just as we have heard from the beginning."

November

✝ *1st November*

Don't allow all that you have accomplished during the warm season of your life, to be stamped out like the burnished leaves of Autumn, which are crushed to a crisp under your feet. Celebrate those little steps that have propelled you into My Kingdom. In heaven they were giant foot prints, that made indentations, into the souls of those I am trying to reach.

Don't underestimate the impact you have in the lives of others, by following My code for living. Be gentle in all your contacts; a smile that puts someone at ease can melt the heart. It can make an opening for Me. You are My representative, so always act with kindness and discipline.

Prayer

Father, open the doors for me to help You reach as many
lost souls as I can. Help me to bring people to You through
seeing Jesus in me and wanting Him for themselves.
Amen.

✝ *2nd November*

Count your blessings. A thankful heart is pleasing to Me. If you begin the day by appreciating all that I have given to you, then the little extra treasures that I give, won't go unnoticed. I supply your needs without the desire to make grand gestures; these are unnecessary for Me to show you My love.

You have a never-ending supply of good things, but don't take them for granted. Because they are always there, it shouldn't make them less valuable to you. There are those among you who have nothing to call their own - people whose daily lives are a struggle. When you count your blessings, count those people among them and share what I have given you.

1 Chronicles 29:13

> *"... everything we have has come from you and we give only what you have already given to us!"*

✝ *3rd November*

I know what is in your mind - your every plan and thought. Don't be distracted by the world and become a slave to selfish ideals. A plan that is prayed about and blessed by Me will succeed beyond your wildest dreams. Listen carefully, for the plans that are wrong for you, will not be blessed.

Your prayers open up a channel for My gentle leading; be ready to stop something, if My Spirit is nudging you. The more you seek Me and want to hear from Me, the clearer the channel will be. My child, you are so impatient to have things under way happen quickly. Sometimes I act instantly, but I am a patient God who sees with wisdom.

1 Chronicles 28:9

"And Solomon my son, get to know your ancestors. Worship and serve him with all your heart and with a willing mind. For the Lord sees every heart and understands and knows every plan and thought. If you seek Him you will find Him. But if you forsake Him, He will reject you forever."

✝ 4th November

Failure comes from not being prepared. Your faith will keep you from planning your 'failure' through lack of trust in Me. In your heart you know I am with you. You know that, with Me and in My strength, you will be strong and courageous.

The more time you spend preparing with Me, the more your confidence will build. I do not promise to remove your fear, but I do promise to help you do things whilst being afraid. My child, look to Me, place your hand in Mine and step out in faith. Together we can do anything!

1 Chronicles 28:20

"... be strong and courageous and do the work. Don't be afraid or discouraged by the size of the task, for The Lord God, my God, is with you. He will not fail you or forsake you."

✝ 5th November

I made all of 'creation'; I did it all out of My goodness and love. Have you ever wondered what the world and 'your life' would be like, if I wasn't a God of love and kindness? You have the promise of My goodness and faithfulness. That is why I expect the same in return from you.

My love endures forever and I quietly wait for your love in return. My chosen people turned away from Me, but Jesus made a way for them and you Gentiles to come to Me freely. Can you turn away from all this love?

1 Chronicles 16:34-36

"Give thanks to the Lord for he is good! His faithful love endures forever. Cry out, save us O God of our salvation! Gather and rescue us from among the nations. So we can thank your holy name and rejoice and praise you. Blessed be the Lord, the God of Israel, from everlasting to everlasting!"

✝ *6th November*

Beware that Satan doesn't warp your perspective. If you are having difficult choices to make, he will try to confuse what you have been taught is right and wrong. My Word will teach you what is morally right. If you have more complex decisions to make, which could have dire consequences, always come to Me!

You must close your ears to Satan's whisperings. You must learn to separate his persuasive lies. Trust Me to direct your path. Do you believe I work everything out for your good? Then trust Me to work out your decisions concerning others, to be for their good also.

Luke 11:17

> *"He knew their thoughts so he said, 'Any kingdom at war with itself is doomed. A divided home is also doomed.' "*

✝ *7th November*

My child, you have a weak spot. It is an area that is most vulnerable and Satan knows about it. He will use it against you and only your strong determination and vigilance will protect you from submitting to his temptations. Jesus was under great stress, from the consistent attacks from Satan during His time in the desert, following His baptism.

You will discover that at your heights of utopia, an opening can occur that will allow Satan in. His lies are intent on stealing your inheritance from you. Scripture will increase your faith and remind you to be forever on your guard.

Hebrews 3:15

"But never forget the warning, 'Today you must listen to his voice. Don't harden your hearts against him as Israel did when they rebelled.'"

✝ 8th November

I have given you the necessary armour to stand up against the darkness of Satan. Don't think yourself a victim who is defenceless. Censure all that he tries to corrupt you with. Make your opposition firm, be strong in My word, as you denounce the 'powers of darkness'.

Have nothing to do with anything that makes you uncomfortable; you are My child and I have planted seeds of knowledge within you to be discerning when something is wrong. My Spirit will warn you in order to prevent any deception. Heed His voice when He speaks!

Hebrews 3:12-13

"Be careful then, dear brothers and sisters. Make sure that your own hearts are not evil and unbelieving, turning you away from the living God. You must warn each other every day, as long as it is called 'today,' so that none of you will be deceived by sin and hardened against God."

✝ 9th November

Before My son took all the sins of the world upon Himself, I punished all sin severely. Sin entered My world through Adam. Satan opened the world up, to become wicked, corrupt and shameful. The severity of My punishments did not halt the evil from reaching epidemic proportions.

Sin has destroyed what was good and eventually destroys relationships and communities. Jesus died to allow those who believe in Him to fight back against the darkness. But the 'day of judgement' will come and all who have not repented and followed Jesus will incur appropriate judgement.

Leviticus 20:7

"So set yourselves apart to be holy, for I the Lord, am your God. Keep all my laws and obey them, for I am the Lord who makes you holy."

✝ 10th November

Medical science has been blessed by Me. Doctors can do all kinds of treatments with the use of blood transfusions that save lifes. Blood can be frozen and stored for future usage in emergencies. But there is no way of sustaining life without it.

That is the reason why the blood that was shed by Jesus is so symbolic. At the last supper, Jesus used bread and wine in a ritual, to explain the new covenant to His disciples. It is a sacred, symbolic act. My Son said, "Do this in remembrance of Me." It is a beautiful, spiritual way to honour Jesus.

Matthew 26:27

> *"And he took a cup of wine and gave thanks to God for it. He gave it to them and said, 'Each of you drink from it, for this is my blood, which seals the covenant, between God and his people. It is poured out to forgive the sins of many.'"*

✝ *11th November*

Jesus was led to His horrific death without uttering a word in His defence. When you are troubled and wanting My intervention, remember His prayer in the garden of Gethsemane. He had a choice, He asked Me to stop His death, but ultimately He accepted My will. He was obedient, despite what He had to face.

Jesus, despite the temptations of this world, remained pure. He could have called down a host of angelic warriors to fight on His behalf, but He remained silent, and accepted all the brutal treatment that should have been your punishment. He is now sitting at My 'right hand', in glory. Doesn't He deserve your unrivalled adoration?

Matthew 26:38-39

"He told them, 'My soul is crushed with grief to the point of death. Stay here and watch with me.' He went on a little farther and fell face down on the ground praying, 'My father if it is possible, let this cup of suffering be taken away from me. Yet I want your will not mine.'"

✝ *12th November*

Peter denied knowing Jesus three times. He was afraid, he knew he would probably be put on trial, with his own subsequent death, if he were to admit knowing Jesus. It is alright to be brave when there will be no repercussions. How would you have answered the question, in the light of a powerful accuser, waiting for your answer?

Peter was ashamed and remembered his Master's words with anguish, just as the cock crowed. But despite his betrayal, Jesus forgave him! You too have been forgiven all your sins! Peter went on to serve Me and helped build the church with Jesus as the Cornerstone. When you are forgiven, My child, it is time for a new start. You have done a wonderful thing by repenting! Now let Me do a new thing in you.

Acts 2:38

"Peter said, 'Each of you must turn from your sins and turn to God and be baptised in the name of Jesus Christ for the forgiveness of your sins. Then you will receive the gift of the Holy Spirit.'"

✝ *13th November*

Your heart is so low, My child. Come to Me and snuggle into My arms. Leave your anger, concern and regrets behind. Tell Me all the things that you are feeling and let Me remove the hurt and pain. It is only by your being honest with Me that I will be able to help you.

The scars of your past are still not healed. If you continue to bury them, I am unable to help. Expose to Me all that you have suffered. I will not be shocked or surprised by your revelations because I already know but I want you to trust Me with your darkest secrets. Tell Me everything and then have complete trust that I will heal you.

Prayer

> *Father, thank you that you care about all of my life. I am placing my hurt and pain at the foot of the cross. All that I have belongs to you and I offer all that I am in return. I am grateful for Your forgiveness and welcome Your healing in my life. Amen.*

✝ 14th November

Some of the things you are still feeling are becoming an obstruction between us. When will you learn to trust Me? How can we be free to become close, unless you are prepared to expose your darkest secrets? Day by day I wait, don't bury these things.

I understand that you are suffering. Some issues seem too personal to disclose. I am the One person that you can trust completely who will keep everything to Myself unconditionally, the only One who can really help you. Will you talk to Me? Will you trust that I am the solution?

Prayer

Father, some things are too painful to talk about, even to You. I want to let them go, but I hold onto them like a child with hidden treasure. Help me to be open with You and to bring everything into the light. In my heart, I know that You are the answer. Amen.

✝ *15th November*

My child, unless a wound is cleaned out completely, it won't heal. Write down your fears, guilt, and deepest secrets, and offer them to Me in prayer. Then delete what you have written. Believe that I have washed and dressed the wounds, and that the area that was festering, is now clean and you are free to heal.

Each time a memory afflicts your mind, disperse it by calling on My name. If you trust Me, slowly at your own speed, these things will recede into the background of your mind. Recalling them will no longer have the intense pain that you have now. Accepting forgiveness for yourself and also forgiving any perpetrator will remove this terrible sadness.

Romans 8:1

"So now there is no condemnation for those who belong to Christ Jesus. For the power of the life-giving spirit has freed you through Christ Jesus from the power of sin that leads to death."

✝ 16th November

Look into your heart and test your opinions. Have you glossed over any of My Word, in order to maintain your present lifestyle? Are you tempted to manipulate what you may consider grey areas, in order to assuage your conscience? Don't rely on your feelings as they will only excuse wrong behaviour and attitudes.

The road remains narrow for you, but you are not resistant enough to outside influences. Be strong and denounce temptations that make your foot slip before the road widens out, into a dual carriageway. There are no such roads on the way to heaven. Take care that you obey the signs and don't start to endorse Satan's slippery rules.

1 Thessalonians 5:19-22

"Do not stifle the Holy Spirit. Do not scoff at prophecies.
But test everything that is said. Hold onto what is good.
Keep away from every kind of evil."

✝ *17th November*

I have planted My Spirit within you, and I long to see you grow this seed to fruit. Ask often for My help, and watch as I nurture you. The change will astound those around you, as you become someone who is spiritually connected to Me. The desires you have now will change as you become purposeful in My Kingdom.

Each of My children have been blessed with a plan for their lives. It will be an exciting journey that unfolds. At every turn there is a promise. The promise is for a better life - a life that will enable you to experience joy for yourself, and also for you to bring joy into the lives of others. Let Me take your life into My hands, and allow Me to help you to develop in this life, so you are fit for the Kingdom to come.

Philippians 1:6

> *"And I am sure that God, who began the good work within you, will continue his work until it is finally finished, on that day when Christ Jesus comes back again."*

✝ 18th November

Patience also requires trust. If you believe that I am involved in your life, then you will wait patiently and with good humour as you endure your circumstances. Look what an opportunity patience gives you to set an example. Draw on this virtue during the many trials you will experience.

My Son came to live among you. He is gentle and accepts the differences between all people. I love you all equally and nothing can change that. Accept all things with trust, patience and fortitude. The darkness you encounter will be overcome by your good attitude which brings light into the darkness. Then, others who don't yet know Me, will see that you are different. You will be My ambassadors.

Romans 12:12

"Be glad for all God is planning for you. Be patient in trouble, and always be prayerful."

✝ 19th November

Be thankful, My child, for your blessings. It is human nature to take them for granted. Look around you and see the poverty and misery that some of My children are going through. Ask Me to help you to develop a grateful heart. The seed of gratitude is present within you but the spirit of selfishness in this world, will whisper to you about your own importance.

Try purposefully to consider others before yourself. You will experience seasons of generosity, but don't allow those feelings of grace to evade you once the season has passed. It should be a daily sacrifice. I have given you enough to be generous at all times. Unless you are counting your own blessings, you will not see just how much you have to share.

Prayer

Father, open my eyes to see the needs of others. Change me so that I am always aware of poverty. Our streets are becoming full of homeless people, and food banks have become a necessity. Give me the courage not to look away, and avoid becoming insulated against the suffering that's in this world. Please don't allow me to ever forget that You have given me enough to share. Amen.

✝ *20th November*

Test what you see and hear, against My Word. Be objective about testimonies; they are hard, if not impossible to disprove. Stories of miraculous signs can be blown out of all proportion. Research these claims and make sure they don't have a satanic influence.

It is better to be considered cynical, rather than to be taken in and exposed to false teaching. You can get a pretty honest view, when you test the heart of someone, against My Word. False teachers may have a natural way of speaking with authority. Ask My Spirit to lead you into all truth.

1 John 4:1

"Dear friends do not believe everyone who claims to speak by the Spirit. You must test them to see if the spirit they have, comes from God. For there are many false prophets in the world."

✝ *21st November*

Your soul controls your carnal desires, but upon accepting Jesus, My Holy Spirit comes to live within your spirit. There is a raging battle between the two, and one must submit to the other. The essence of My Spirit is to empower you to overcome your human desires.

Your lustful materialism, that craves self-satisfaction and is present in your soul, must be controlled by you! Your sin will cause My Spirit to be grieved within your heart. A submissive, penitent attitude will appease and renew our relationship. I see the fight you have, My child, and I will reward and empower your determined battle.

2 Corinthians 4:16-17

"That is why we never give up. Though our bodies are dying, our spirits are being renewed every day."

✝ *22nd November*

Mercy matters now more than ever. My mercy responds in compassion and forgiveness - towards all of My children who come to Me in repentance. My grace is unmerited favour towards someone when it is within My power to punish and I chose to forgive. My child you have access to the Divine plan of redemption.

My Son died not for the righteous, but for sinners. So My forgiveness is based on love and reconciliation, through the blood of Jesus. We therefore have a 'maternal' connection and I am your Father. My mercy joins all My children together as My church.

Romans 6:17-18

"Thank God once you were slaves of sin, but now you have obeyed with all your heart the new teaching God has given you. Now you are free from sin your old master and you have become slaves to your new master, righteousness."

✝ *23rd November*

I long to hear your prayers. Immediately you speak, we are together. I hear the depths of your despair, the cries of your heart, even before you speak. It releases joy in heaven, as soon as you bow your head. Remember your first love and the happiness you felt when they got in touch? In the same way My heart jumps with gladness, when you call to Me.

The quiet times we have together, which are sometimes emotional, when you bring your worries and subsequent requests, are momentous occasions. Your heart is vulnerable and open to Me. I am able to respond in a personal way, because of our close Spiritual connection. Come, My child, and be honest with Me - tell me what you need.

2 Chronicles 7:15-16

> *"I will listen to every prayer made in this place. For I*
> *have chosen this Temple and set it apart to be my home*
> *forever. My eyes and my heart will always be here."*

✝ 24th November

Your deep thoughts trouble you. Unless you express them to Me, I cannot help. Sometimes you treat each day, in such a rigid way, without seeing the benefits of sharing with Me. I will not intrude where an unwelcome attitude exists. Why, after all that we have been through together, do you still sometimes shut Me out?

Do you still not recognise the advantages of seeking My presence? Do your choices satisfy you? Are you confident to work things out alone? I am here, I want you to pause, notice Me and request My input. Look at the difference when you consult with Me, My child. Don't forget that now you have the Helper.

John 10:2-4

"For a shepherd enters through the gate. The gate keeper opens the gate for him and the sheep hear his voice and come to him. He calls his own sheep by name and leads them out. After he has gathered his own flock, he walks ahead of them and they follow him because they recognise his voice."

✝ 25th November

The cross has brought you freedom. Visualise the now empty place that brought defeat over death. My Son's body was taken down, wrapped in burial clothes, a stone rolled over the entrance to the tomb where His dead body was placed. On the third day He was resurrected! Nothing could contain His victory!

The world has a way out of its sin! Anyone, anyone at all, who believes that Jesus is My Son, and that He has taken the sins of the world upon Himself, they will be accepted, in forgiveness, as a member of My family. They are now My precious children whom I love!

John 1:29

"The next day John saw Jesus coming toward him and said, 'Look! There is the lamb of God who takes away the sin of the world.'"

✝ *26th November*

You are very special to Me! Very precious and nothing in the world will be allowed to separate you from Me. I hear your praises, I see all your attempts to serve Me and I welcome your prayers. There is never a time when I am too busy to listen to you.

I appreciate every effort you make on My behalf. The longings of your heart are known to Me and I will make each of your requests a priority. Be constantly expectant when you have consulted Me about something. In My perfect timing, things will begin to happen.

Micah 7:7

"As for me I look to the Lord for his help. I wait confidently for God to save me and my God will certainly hear me."

✝ *27th November*

Physical healing is a necessary part of My ministry to you. I use many different ways to achieve this. Numerous are My instruments. I like to diversify and surprise you. You try, but you can never second guess Me, so why not leave the arrangements and the ultimate outcome with Me.

Just trust with a deep, unquestioning, faith and have no fear. Can you do that, My child? Read all the scriptures on healing and note the varying methods that are used. Note the strong, accepting faith, that is essential for you to be healed. So come with your requests, come in trust and obedience and wait with patience and believe.

Psalm 27:14

"Wait patiently for the Lord. Be brave and courageous.
Yes, wait patiently for the Lord."

✝ 28th November

I require you to have a grateful heart, no matter what life throws at you. Whatever trials and tribulations you encounter along the way, keep your eyes fixed on Me and be prepared to accept them. I will not allow anything to happen in your life, without providing whatever is necessary for you to survive it with victory.

I reward obedience, I strengthen you when you trust Me and carry on when the outcome looks bleak. I will uplift that outpouring of grief from your heart, as you cry out to Me in despondency. I will build up your character and make you into a new person.

Isaiah 43:18-19

"But forget all that - it is nothing compared to what I am going to do. For I am about to do a brand new thing. See I have already begun! Do you not see it?"

✝ *29th November*

I want to expand your faith. Take hold of My hand and look straight ahead until your eyes can no longer focus. The future looks uncertain to you, because you can no longer see the outcome. I am at every junction of the road and your wobbly steps will grow stronger, as you gain courage, along the way.

I will award you 'gold medals' of encouragement. Look out for them as they take many different forms. Wether words of praise or promotion, helping hands to speed you on or signs of success, they will be found in the treasures that I lay out for you along the way. Stay righteous in Me, so your integrity will remain intact. Hear My words – "you good and faithful servant!"

2 Chronicles 16:9

"The eyes of the Lord search the whole earth in order to strengthen those whose hearts are fully committed to him."

✝ *30th November*

The twists and turns of life are making your journey interesting. Enjoy the obstacles, as you pit your brain against these diversions. Look upon them as little tests of achievement, that stimulate your spiritual growth. I like to stretch you, as I gently lead and teach, in ways that are unknown and extraordinary.

Our journey is so exciting and sometimes the unexpected results carry you along in a different direction to the one I had planned. Sometimes we will run with it, but on other occasions, I will gently turn you back, to a more definite, suitable route. Don't be afraid - things are always under My control.

Revelation 3:8

"I know all the things you do and I have opened a door for you, that no one can shut. You have little strength, yet you obeyed my word and did not deny me."

December

✝ 1st December

I have ultimate control of the world and the outcome is already ordained. My promise is for My children to have eternal life. If this life brings you suffering, you must remain faithful, only then will your faith prove genuine.

Remind each other during these trials about My promises. I will not fail you, so follow Christ and hold on to the certainty of your eternal life.

Revelation 2:10

> *"Don't be afraid of what you are about to suffer. The Devil will throw some of you into prison and put you to the test. You will be persecuted for ten days. Remain faithful even when facing death and I will give you the crown of life."*

✝ 2nd December

I appeared to a virgin and told her she would give birth to My Son. Mary accepted what I said and gave birth to the Saviour of the world. Mary's simple trust empowered her life. She faced a hostile world, with a humiliating, secret pregnancy. Her reputation was a secondary concern, in her desire to obey Me.

Are you prepared today, to do whatever I could ask of you? Your comfortable life might be disturbed, all the things you hold dear could be taken from you? When you renew your covenant vows at the start of each new year, do you really listen to what you are saying?

Luke 1:34-35

> *"Mary asked the Angel, 'But how can I have a baby, I am a virgin?' The Angel replied, 'The Holy Spirit will come upon you and the power of the Most High will overshadow you. So the baby born to you will be holy and he will be called the Son of God.'"*

✝ *3rd December*

My faithful servants, Mary and Joseph, travelled to Bethlehem to register for the census, in the town of Joseph's birth. They became refugees for Me, their future was unknown to them. With a young child, they learnt they had to escape in fear for their lives. Do you think they regretted saying Yes to Me?

When you follow Me, your path won't necessarily be a smooth road. There will be many, many bumps in it, but we will ride those obstacles together. The journey will be rewarding and revealing and if you travel with a trusting heart, it will be enjoyable.

2 Corinthians 3:16-17

"But whenever anyone turns to the Lord, the veil is taken away. Now the Lord is the Spirit and wherever the Spirit of the Lord is, he gives freedom."

✝ *4th December*

Elizabeth and Zachariah had their son, John the Baptist, when they were very old. Elizabeth had passed the age of child bearing. His initial doubts led to My preventing Zachariah from speaking, until John was born. Zachariah's eventual obedience allowed him to speak again, when he agreed to John's name. They had yearned for a child for so long, but My timing was perfect.

If you grow weary of waiting for what you desire, remember the miracle of John's birth. It is never too late! I can work as you exercise patience and trust. I can make 'your' endurance an example to others and you will receive many blessings when you believe. Ask Me in faith for what you want, never doubting My desire to give to you.

Romans 8:25

> *"But if we look forward to something we don't have yet,*
> *we must wait patiently and confidently."*

✝ 5th December

Mary treasured all the joy in her heart when she was told by the angel that she would give birth to Jesus. She was a humble, young girl who because of her unquestioning obedience, brought Jesus into this cold, hostile world. Could you have laid your fears aside and agreed to that selfless act? It was unthinkable to have a baby outside of marriage, at that time.

The depth of her trust made it possible for Jesus to enter this world, to be born into a loving family, as the son of a carpenter. How much would you trust Me, if I were to ask something unthinkable of you?

Luke 1:38

"Mary responded, 'I am the Lords servant and I am willing to accept whatever he wants. May everything you have said come true.' And then the Angel left."

✝ *6th December*

John the Baptist prepared the way for Jesus. I have sent people before you all of your life, to get you ready, for the time when you would surrender to Me. You have been exposed to children's prayers by a parent or in Sunday School. Look back and there was always someone in your life who was showing you the way.

Not all of My children were blessed with a Christian parent, but at some stage in your life, you will have had the opportunity of hearing My Word. Don't be like the heathens who have rejected Me. At some point in your journey, you will be expected to make a decision. Please, My child, make it an informed one.

Proverbs 18:15

"Intelligent people are always open to new ideas, in fact they look for them."

✝ *7th December*

My child, I see the extra work you impose upon yourself because of what the world has chosen as My Son's birthday. My Word is full of descriptions of celebrations and I delight in this season. To bring joy to another by offering them a gift is a wonderful way to celebrate the birth of My Son.

But, My precious child, do not go overboard. Do not cause yourself to be in debt. The celebration is about My gift of Jesus to you! Praise, with a thankful heart, is a fitting tribute. Make sure the presence of this materialistic society doesn't cloud the joy of the of the season. Be thankful and celebrate the birth of My Son, in your own special way.

Luke 2:30-32

"I have seen the saviour you have given to all people. He is a light to reveal God to all nations and he is the glory of your people Israel."

✝ 8th December

The season brings good humour and much merriment, even to those who are not Christians. It is a joyful time, but also a dangerous time. It's an opportunity for parties and an even bigger relaxation of your morals. Guard your good intentions from compromise and failure. Beware of flirtatious behaviour.

I see all that goes on including the things you would rather I didn't see. Regrettable things can happen particularly at parties. They start off in innocence, but can quickly escalate when your discernment is clouded by the merriment of the season.

Proverbs 6:32

"But the man who commits adultery is an utter fool, for he destroys his own soul."

✝ 9th December

Flattery is often used in sexual temptation. It is a complex area of the human character, don't be too conceited as to believe all the compliments that are heaped upon you. Many are the silver tongued words used to entice an unwilling participant, into immoral behaviour.

I will strengthen you in your weaknesses. Be careful not to allow yourself to be put into vulnerable settings, where you are alone, with the opposite sex. Many struggle to resist, that velvet tongue.

Proverbs 7:21-23

So she seduced him with her pretty speech. With her flattery she enticed him. He followed her at once, like an ox going to the slaughter or like a trapped stag awaiting the arrow that would pierce his heart. He was like a bird flying into a snare, little knowing it would cost him his life.

✝ 10th December

Remember those who are less fortunate than yourself, not just in this holiday season of celebration, but also for the rest of the year. It is better to give with an attitude of wanting to help, rather than with guilt for being blessed with more than they have.

You are a steward of My money and I like it when you ask Me where I would like you to give. I see where the greatest need is and I will guide you in that direction. Circumstances may have made the poor act in a certain way, but leave Me to do the judging.

2 Corinthians 8:7

"You must each make up your own mind as to how much you should give. Don't give reluctantly or in response to pressure. For God loves the person who gives cheerfully."

✝ *11th December*

The season of praise is upon you. Carols are being sung, and little ones are getting excited at the coming of Christmas. I love all this joy, the compassion that is coming out in the most unexpected places. Oh, would that it could be like this all the year round! How much more would the world be reached for Christ if my people loved each other consistently throughout the year.

The harmony that the seed of Christmas brings, is so uplifting to your soul. My child, continue to spread these seeds throughout the rest of the year. Jesus came that you would live like this always.

1 Peter 4:8

"Most important of all, continue to show deep love for each other, for love covers a multitude of sins."

✝ *12th December*

Stop during all this busyness and count your blessings. Have you money in your purse, food on your table, a church family, a Bible? Most of all, My child, you have Me! Our time together is most important!

Events in your life sometimes cause you to let time with Me slide. You can speak to me anywhere as I am always waiting, listening and ready to have you consciously aware of Me. How can I communicate with you if you don't first give Me your attention? My will is for there to be an open line between us – one which is strong and sensitive. Open it up, My child.

Psalm 65:4

> *"What joy for those you choose to bring near, those who live in your Holy courts. What joy awaits us inside your Holy temple."*

✝ *13th December*

My Son is your Advocate and the Intercessor between us. Set your heart to do My will and seek My face. I long so much for you, My child! Practice coming into My revealing presence. Slow obedience is a form of disobedience. I want you to obey Me quickly. I want you to get to know My heart.

Only by spending time with Me can we develop this intimate relationship. It is your will that prevents it. Start to demonstrate this priority in your life. Don't have the presumptive attitude that our friendship won't need commitment from you.

Isaiah 55:6

"Seek the Lord while you can find him. Call on him now while he is near."

✝ 14th December

It is only right that I have given you boundaries. As we grow in our closeness, you will begin to appreciate them and they will become a security for you. Boundaries protect what is inside them; but remember, they also protect and stop what's on the outside from coming in. Satan will try to break down your boundaries.

The more familiar you are with My Word and the more obedient you are to Me, the easier it will be to stay within those limits. When you become tempted by what is on the outside, you must heed those dangerous signals. Ask for My strength and speak out My promises.

1 Corinthians 10:13

"... He will keep the temptation from becoming so strong that you can't stand up against it. When you are tempted he will show you a way out so that you will not give into it."

✝ *15th December*

I see all of My children as equal. I love you all to the same degree. Not one of you is of more value to Me, than another. I want you to live your lives in this way and think of no one as better or worse than yourself. All your different gifts and abilities come from the same Spirit!

If you do anything for Me, it is of great value in My Kingdom, because you are all part of My body, the church. Each has an important part to do and works together with the rest of the members. My child, never undervalue or compare your gifts with another's. Work to the very best of your ability and I will be pleased by your service.

1 Corinthians 12:5-7

"There are different kinds of service in the church, but it is the same Lord who we are serving. There are different ways that God works in our lives, but it is the same God who does the work through all of us. A spiritual gift is given to us as a means of helping the entire church."

✝ *16th December*

My Spirit's desire for unity will bond you to other Christians. You will want to have fellowship with them. The diversity of the members of My church is what makes your working together uniquely satisfying.

I did not intend any uniformity when I blessed you with abilities. As you work and use your individual gifts it will complement the whole body. Relax into your qualities and allow Me to make them excellent.

1 Corinthians 12:12-13

"The human body has many parts, but many parts make up only one body. So it is with the body of Christ. Some of us are Jews, some are Gentiles, some are slaves and some are free. But we have all been baptised into Christ's body by one spirit and we have all received the same Spirit."

✝ *17th December*

My love is unfailing! Material things break or wear out but My deep love for you goes on and on, no matter what you do. I cannot look upon sin, but My Son intercedes on your behalf. When you get on a downward spiral and feel separated from Me, just keep whispering 'Jesus.' I will join you in the darkness.

I hear your cries and My Spirit groans on your behalf. Depression brings an overwhelming sense of loneliness, often accompanied by self-loathing. Don't assume that your distress separates you from Me! If you will allow it to, it will bring us closer.

Psalm 136:23-26

> *"He remembered our utter weakness. His faithful love endures forever. He saved us from our enemies. His faithful love endures forever. He gives food to every living thing. His faithful love endures forever. Give thanks to the God of heaven."*

✝ 18th December

Your mind, if you allow Me to train it, can become a fertile place of peace. When you readily read My Word, I will bring you great understanding. It will make you hunger for Me. I am behind each Word and only I can quench your thirst. Open your Bible with a determination to read with new insight.

I will teach you the principles of My law and you will come to love it. Study small portions of it and take the privilege of these words into your heart. It is the only sure way of truly learning who I really am.

Psalm 119:164-167

"I will praise you seven times a day because all your laws are just. Those who love your law have great peace and do not stumble. I long for your salvation Lord so I have obeyed your commands. I have obeyed your decrees and I love them very much."

✝ *19th December*

Do you have sickness or injury? Do you believe that I can heal you? You need an in-depth knowledge of Me and an open mind to really believe that miracles can and do happen today. My ultimate desire is for your heart to be right with Me. Your body takes second place because it's your soul that I want to be at one with.

I do not want to see you in pain, as I see the destructive thoughts which can result. It is sometimes necessary for you to suffer a while, in order to build up your strength in Me. I look always into the heart and soul. Physical healing will need great faith from you, are you ready to believe Me for it? I sometimes work through medical professionals but My children always want instant results.

Luke 5:12-13

> *"... when the man saw Jesus he fell to the ground, face down in the dust, begging to be healed. 'Lord,' he said, 'If you want to you can make me well again.' Jesus reached out and touched the man. 'I want to,' He said, 'Be healed.'"*

✝ 20th December

Examine the healing miracles of My Son. Some required some action, on the part of the person asking for healing. You must seek Me with all your heart; you must believe, without a shadow of doubt and you must trust Me. During the time of the early church, there were many miraculous signs.

Why do you not face this life here and now with expectancy? My power in the world is gaining momentum, despite the fact that Satan is slithering into many more areas. My Christian soldiers are fighting back. Are you one of them?

Thought

There are many grey areas in our understanding of God's plans. We organise in our minds the way we would address issues and then expect that God will comply. Do you suggest the way you think God should solve your problems? Are you upset when He doesn't conform. He probably feels the same way about us.

✝ *21st December*

When you read about the faith of others in My Word and their subsequent victory, does your lack of faith frighten you? When you follow Me despite your difficulties, it expresses your faith. Trusting Me and enduring when you have no idea of the outcome, shows your faith. The faith that you have in My provision, opens doors for more to be released.

I can rekindle the smallest amount of faith and you, even not knowing all the answers, will develop it. When you face adversity, it will destroy counterfeit faith. Your personal faith affects others. There is a difference between faith and belief; waiting with trust will strengthen you. It is faith not perfection that makes you right in My eyes. I want to see if you are willing to obey Me.

Genesis 15:6

> *"... and Abram believed the Lord and the Lord declared him righteous because of his faith."*

✝ *22nd December*

Be wary of outside pressure which can push you into conforming to the world's values. It is very difficult for you to speak out against the majority and their loud voices. A righteous person would do so. Ask Me to strengthen you to be able to stand up for what is right.

I will give you a heart of compassion and make you steadfast against the dilution of social responsibility. Be upright and honourable, truthful and courageous, in your fight for justice.

Exodus 23:2

"Do not join a crowd that intends to do evil. When you are on the witness stand, do not be swayed in your testimony by the opinion of the majority."

✝ *23rd December*

If you are not continually correcting the way you live your life, your values will easily succumb to the world's values that are being followed by unbelievers. Social pressures are a very real temptation and unless you are vigilant in your determination to live your life with integrity according to My Word, it will be a very slippery slope.

Destruction comes in all guises. 'Just once' is rarely that and you're vulnerable to start forming habits that will lead to the wrong path. If you faithfully give these temptations to Me, I will keep correcting you until they become temptations no more.

Exodus 23:24

> *"Do not worship the gods of these other nations or serve them in any way and never follow their evil example. Instead, you must utterly conquer them and break down their shameful idols."*

✝ *24th December*

Remember there are many lonely people who won't see anyone tomorrow. They may say, "Well, it's just another day," but you know that it is not. Draw on your fruit of compassion and try to include them in your happy family unit. Very few people would choose to be on their own in this season of merriment.

Don't be fooled though that everyone except you is having a good time. It is the most lonely time of the year, when loved ones are especially missed; when memories cause nostalgia and can upset even the most hardened hearts. Look out for those who are suffering just because it's Christmas.

1 Kings 19:4

"Then he went on alone into the desert, travelling all day. He sat down under a solitary broom tree and prayed that he might die. 'I have had enough Lord,' he said. 'Take my life for I am no better than my ancestors.' "

✝ *25th December*

Revel in the joy of the birth of My Son! Share this gladness with all. Make today a new beginning that will cause your heart to overflow with love. Think of Jesus - the tiny, wriggling baby, wrapped in Mary's arms of love. His future was sealed from the time of her acceptance of being His mother.

Let today be about His birth and the hope that He brought to the world. Show by your example how His sacrificial life, has made a difference to yours.

Luke 2:10-12

> *"But the Angel reassured them. 'Don't be afraid,' he said, 'I bring you news of great joy for everyone! The Saviour - yes the Messiah, the Lord has been born tonight in Bethlehem, the City of David! And thus is how you will recognise him. You will find a baby lying in a manger, wrapped snugly in strips of cloth!'"*

✝ *26th December*

My Spirit came upon you at the moment of your re-birth. I have lived in you ever since. I have fed and nurtured you, just as a mother takes care of her child. I constantly watch over your days and My Spirit gently guides you.

You are growing in the qualities that I have placed within you and in time, be in no doubt, you will reach maturity. We have a long, narrow road to travel before then. I want you to enjoy the journey, to feel secure in My love and protection.

Exodus 33:12-13

"… you call me by name and tell me I have found favour with you. Please if this is really so, show me your intentions so I will understand you more fully and do exactly what you want me to do."

✝ *27th December*

The more I have blessed you with, the more responsibility to be a good steward will fall upon your shoulders. What abilities do you have? Look at the gifts that I have given you. Are you prepared to use them in helping others? Be always on the lookout for people who are in need.

How much spare money have you got, are you sharing it with those less fortunate than yourself? The way you handle and disperse modest resources, reflects an accurate picture of your heart.

2 Kings 4:8-10

"One day Elisha went to the town of Shunem. A wealthy woman lived there and she invited him in to eat some food. From then on, whenever he passed that way he would stop there to eat. She said to her husband, 'I am sure this man who stops in from time to time, is a holy man of God. Let's make a little room for him on the roof and furnish it with a bed, a table, a chair and a lamp. Then he will have a place to stay whenever he comes by.'"

✝ 28th December

Are you having to count the cost of over spending during the Christmas period? Materialism can distort your ideals. Adverts for the next best, biggest, most desirable 'things' can corrupt your senses. Be wary of thinking that by acquiring these 'things', they will make you happy.

All of them are 'nine day wonders'! Very soon you will move on to the next advert telling you what you 'need.' Eventually you will recognise that nothing that will perish can satisfy you. I am what you need. Take time in prayer, My child, and offer up all that you have and all that you want to Me.

Prayer

Father, when the glitz and the glamour overtake my common sense, bring me back to earth. You are all I want, so forgive me for overlooking that basic instinct in my life.
Amen.

✝ 29th December

During the year you have had many ups and downs. Thank you for sharing all of those times with Me. You have grown during our time together and I see you are reaching new heights of understanding. Your increased commitment to Me, has shown a heart that is true and kind.

You have diligently tried to remain faithful and I appreciate that our relationship has become closer. Continue to study the areas where you are weakest and I will constantly strengthen you. Come to Me quickly, when you are afraid and remember that nothing that concerns you is too small to concern Me.

1 Peter 2:9

"But you are not like that, for you are a chosen people.
You are a kingdom of priests, God's holy nation, his very
own possession. This is so you can show others the goodness
of God, for he called you out of the darkness into his
wonderful light."

✝ 30th December

As this year is coming to an end, take stock of the changes in your life that have occurred. Some things have brought you low and I have had to work to bring you through them. Never worry about being alone because I am always, always with you!

Don't rely on your feelings so much - they truly can't be trusted. Set your mind to have a joyful, positive attitude and be constantly in charge of your rampant thoughts. Love each other, even through the hurts. Don't be easily offended, but reach out to your enemies in love. I will give you the grace to do this.

1 Peter 2:1-3

"So get rid of all malicious behaviour and deceit. Don't just pretend to be good! Be done with hypocrisy and jealousy and backstabbing. You must crave pure spiritual milk so that you can grow into the fullness of your salvation. Cry out for this nourishment, as a baby cries out for milk, now that you have had a taste of the Lord's kindness."

✝ *31st December*

A Prayer to God

My dearest Father, I can never repay what Jesus has done for me, or the sacrifice You have both made. The mysteries of the Trinity are deeply hidden from me, but I revel in discovering more and more of Your character. I will soak up Your presence between the pages of Your Word.

Show me all the precious gifts that you have blessed me with. Teach me to unravel them and knit them into something special within Your Kingdom. I want my face to express the joy you have placed in my heart. I want to be on fire for You, so that others will want to know You too.

Thank You for Your love and provision, for upholding me, and, for Your guidance through many adversities during the last year. I am grateful for the hope You have placed in my heart. As I become more committed to You, I will look forward to the future.

Give me a heart that will please You, make me sensitive

and discerning, always eagerly ready to forgive and turn away from my real tendency to sin. I am so grateful to You, for ensuring that when You called to me, I heard you.

In Jesus' name, thank you!

Amen.